EVERYTHING TENANTS NEED TO KNOW TO GET THEIR MONEY'S WORTH

EVERYTHING TENANTS NEED TO KNOW TO GET THEIR MONEY'S WORTH

□

The Compleat Guide to Tenanting for Apartment, Townhouse, Co-op, and Condominium Dwellers

□

RUTH REJNIS

David McKay Company, Inc.

NEW YORK

To my mother and father

Contents

EVERYTHING TENANTS NEED TO KNOW TO GET THEIR MONEY'S WORTH

CHAPTER 1

☐

Portrait of the Tenant

In olden days (thirty years ago), folklore placed apartment people a shade higher on the social scale than the thoroughly disreputable "trailer camp" resident, but far, far below the respectable homeowner. There was something so temporary about tenants, so fleeting. They simply did not count. By their very ease of mobility they could not be depended on to stay around and stabilize a community or contribute much to its betterment. Naturally they were improvident as well, or they would own a house.

Renters could be pasted with two labels: shiftless fly-by-nights —gangsters, for instance, and scatty show business people—or touchingly-poor-but-honest types, families like the Nolans in *A Tree Grows in Brooklyn*, whose poverty tied them to the jumbled tenements of the big cities.

There were a few exceptions to the stigma. Storeowners were allowed to live in quarters above their businesses. Apartments were also accepted for single people who had no need for a large house. Not young single people though. *They* remained at home until they married. Newlyweds were also permitted to rent. It was assumed that within a year or two, with a fatter bank account in hand—and probably a baby in arms—they would be off to their niche in picket fencedom.

The rush to own one's home, further accelerating the disparagement of the renter, reached a peak in the years following World War II when a great migration, led by William Levitt and other construction pipers, headed for a new Xanadu: the suburban tract house. Homeowning became an even shinier goal, but now the house had to be a small, sleek ranch or split level on a fifth of an acre of land, far from the increasingly maddening city.

Single-family homebuilding continued for the next twenty years at an astounding rate (from 900,000 to 1 million plus new houses every year since 1947), but then in the mid-1960s an interesting new housing phenomenon introduced itself. In a typical American about-face, what was once unfashionable now became an accepted, even chic, way to live. Psychologists theorize that the dawn of what is still the apartment era can be traced principally to the evolution of the American home unit during that time. The so-called "extended family" splintered. Where once three or more generations lived unquestioningly under the same roof, a different housing style emerged. Old, urban dwellings were being torn down for center city commercial expansion. And in burgeoning suburbia it was difficult to make room for a grandparent or uncle or even an extra member of one's own generation in compact, pared-to-the-bone subdivision houses that had none of the space of those rambling homesteads back in town.

Expectations, even demands, also changed. The elderly were living longer—and in apartments. Young people were remaining unmarried a few more years into their twenties. They wanted apartments. Many more jobs required a mobility of their holders, keeping them tied by the relatively light bonds of apartment leases rather than mortgage payments. Everyone, regardless of age, began to want freedom, as the now strangely nostalgic phrase put it, "to do his own thing." There was work to dig into, new leisure time activities, protest, hobbies, courses, politics. And for those who wanted even more change, there was divorce. In 1968 the divorce rate rose from 2.9 per 1000 population to 4.3 for the first nine months of 1973. At least one-half of those fractured couples usually took refuge in an apartment.

So off they all went—at least those who had the means—stepping to the tune of a variety of drummers. Grandmother's path took her to a Florida condominium. Mother and Dad, with the children gone, settled in an adult community. Older Brother married. His wife and one child, forming the new, smaller "nuclear family," bought a townhouse operating under the condominium form of ownership. Single-family houses had rapidly been priced out of their means. Sister moved to a singles complex. Younger Brother is still in college, living, naturally, in an off-campus apartment. It is unlikely he will return to live at home after graduation. How many do?

As it was once imperative that every member of the family have his own television set and car and telephone, now it sometimes seems there must be a separate apartment for each of them too—everyone into his own little isolating warren. Could families spanning several generations ever manage to live together again as they did a relatively few years ago? Not many try.

Homeowning is still the ideal and single-family construction has exploded since the post-war years, but apartment construction began to experience its own impressive spurt. Builders, in the true entrepreneurial spirit, were ready to answer the plea for thousands of additional apartment units (individual apartments within one building or complex). In 1973 there were 797,000 new apartment starts vs. 325,000 in 1966, according to statistics compiled by the Advance Mortgage Corporation, a Detroit subsidiary of the First National City Corporation. And the year 1974, the National Association of Home Builders predicted, would see apartment construction surpass that of single-family houses for the first time. Where fourteen years ago 75 percent of the population lived in single-family houses, the 1970 census showed that now one-third of the population resides in multi-unit dwellings. "Demand is so strong that you could almost leave out the bathroom and rent a new apartment," reported one pleased but amazed California developer.

And the prospective renter now has the choice of becoming a city or country person. Apartment buildings do not spring up only in the inner city. Builders have found in recent years that due to land scarcity and the high cost of both land and building materials, it is more economically feasible to build suburban apartment communities rather than single-family developments. Apartment hunters like that idea too. Where the suburbs were once almost exclusively private homes, they are now 45 percent apartment complexes, a growing number of them condominiums and townhouses.

Almost more important than the actual presence of apartments, and their popularity, has been the acceptance of the housing style as . . . well, a respectable one. Apartment living, at least for the middle- and upper-income dwellers who have control over where they will live, has now reached the plane of permanency, responsibility, and affluence that had been associated only with homeowning.

Plain envy enters the picture, too. The newer communities, competing to attract occupants, dangle the latest amenities before apartment hunters. There are swimming pools, tennis courts, game rooms, saunas, social programs. How many single-family homeowners, choking on mortgage payments and ever-climbing maintenance and property taxes, can afford to live like that? And how can they afford to look down on those who do?

Suburban householders who equated apartments with lower property values, crowded schools, and higher taxes were also in for a surprise. Apartment people do not necessarily bring those pestilences along with them. Planners in St. Louis County, Missouri, where apartments account for about 60 percent of all new residential construction, made a study of tenants to see just how well-founded suburban fears were. The report showed St. Louis apartment dwellers had fewer children than residents of single-family homes and so could hardly be jamming the schools.

The tenants also had lower police-protection needs, street maintenance, and other public service costs than a single-family subdivision on the same acreage. Finally, the study found that commercial development, bringing more tax revenue to the area, often follows the location of new apartment complexes. Conclusion: no noticeable difference between owners and renters. If anything, tenants were slightly less burdensome to the community.

Recognition of tenants, especially the buying power their numbers represented, extended to the consumer field. Where apartment dwellers once had to gain what how-to hints they could from such magazines as *House Beautiful* and *House and Garden*, today there are at least two national publications dedicated to the unique decorating problems of the apartment dweller. Furniture makers have also become aware of the rental market. Although they are still manufacturing massive, multi-piece dining room sets and winding living room sectionals for the homeowner, it is now possible to purchase smaller-scaled furnishings to fit sometimes Lilliputian apartment living rooms and dining "L"s. Besides being smaller and of lighter weight, the new renters' furniture is easily transportable and can function, chameleonlike, in several different rooms, if one is fortunate enough to *have* several different rooms. Rental furniture is another new development and one that has proven a boon to the mobile tenant.

Academics and others interested in housing have never been able to decide which is the better mode of living: to buy or to rent. The family that rents, they point out, has more control over living expenses because the charges are fixed; there is no loss on one's investment and no commitment for payment on a mortgage; renting is more flexible in that it is easier to move and try another part of town or even another town. On the other hand, owning a home still represents a certain measure of success. It is a good investment and a fairly safe one. The homeowner's property will almost certainly increase in value and be sold for a profit. Owning is a hedge against inflation; there are tax advantages; a family can make any changes to the house and grounds it can afford; whatever money has been paid in toward the mortgage is forced savings and may be used as security should an emergency loan be needed.

Sylvia Porter, in one of her consumer columns, pointed out that in the five-year period from 1967 to 1972 the cost of renting rose 19 percent, while the cost of home ownership (mortgage interest rates, property taxes and insurance, maintenance and repairs) rose 40 percent. Those figures do not, of course, include the year 1973 when the really backbreaking increases took place. Although she admits there is no simple yes or no to the buy/rent question, Ms. Porter does say that in the long run, if one plans to stay put, it is cheaper to buy—either a single-family house or an apartment—than to rent. For those who are undecided where to settle or are in highly mobile jobs or are unable to afford the escalating cost of ownership, there is no choice: They rent.

The disadvantages of both living styles can run to as lengthy a list as the pluses. The homeowner is required to lay out a hefty amount for a down payment these days, sometimes as much as 30 percent of purchase price. Extended over a period of thirty years, mortgage payments are an added, seemingly eternal, burden. And the care of a house goes on and on. Maintenance can become a drag and repairs are time consuming and, like everything else these days, increasingly costly. Homeowners sometimes have a long wait for a buyer when they want to sell and, depending on the vagaries of the economy at the time, may have to take a loss when they finally find one.

Renters have a different litany of frustrations: constant, tiresome haggling with the landlord to get necessary repairs made; escalating rents; small, crowded units; lack of privacy; noise pollution and the flimsy construction of many apartment buildings. But the biggest regret of tenants over their choice of housing is watching all that rent money go down the drain with nothing to show for it. For example, a monthly check to the landlord for $175 adds up to $2100 a year.

But lately there has even been an answer to that gnawing sense of waste. In the early 1970s, the condominium and the cooperative emerged. Many consider them the best of both housing worlds. They offer two different styles of apartment *ownership*. Cooperatives, where one buys shares in the corporation that owns the building, have made impressive gains in the last ten or so years. No one private or governmental agency is certain of exact construction statistics, but the Cooperative League of the USA, a nationwide organization of all kinds of co-ops, appears to have the most definitive figures. They estimate there were about 800 housing cooperatives in the country in 1972, with more than 500,000 individual members. "We're suspicious of that figure though," said a spokesman for CLUSA. "We think it's low." Still, the housing method showed a neat gain from the 497 co-ops in existence in 1961 with their 121,000 members.

If the cooperative story is one of modestly successful gains, condominium development has taken off like a second stage rocket. The federal government now expects half the population to live in them within the next twenty years. In the condominium method buyers purchase their apartments outright, much in the manner of a single-family house. Statisticians have not been breaking down apartment construction into rental, condominium or cooperative units, so again exact figures are hard to come by. But again it is possible to chart the increase as nearly accurately as possible. The National Association of Home Builders estimates that 69 percent of all multifamily units constructed in 1973 were condominiums. The Advance Mortgage Corporation expected 250,000 or more condo starts in 1973 (exact figures have not yet been compiled). That compared with 235,000 units in 1972, 80,000 in 1971, and 40,000 in 1970.

Housing officials and academics contend that apartment ownership is the wave of the future for economic and land conservation reasons. Certainly renting is not, although by far the majority of America's 70 million apartment dwellers ($\frac{3}{5}$ of the non-white population and $\frac{1}{3}$ of the white population) are presently renting. Construction of rental units was down in 1973 (as was single-family homebuilding; only condos showed a gain), and it was not just because of high construction prices and the overall housing malaise. As James C. Downs, board chairman of Chicago's Real Estate Research Corporation, commented in a trade publication: "It doesn't pay to build rental property anymore, in any areas of the country. Rental properties are obsolete in an inflationary economy. You simply cannot make any money on them because rents are too low and you can't raise rents fast enough to keep up with the rising costs."

Rent controls, where they are in existence, are another bane, landlords contend. How can you set a ceiling on one portion of the economy, they ask, when there is none on the factors making up that rate (fuel costs, taxes and so forth)?

The reason for abandoning rental building is not merely a dollars-and-cents one. The landlord–tenant relationship, always a distrustful one, has, in the last five years, turned especially sour and venomous. Its basic tenet—the lord of the land and his powerless vassals—everyone agrees is outdated and increasingly unworkable. By their very transience, some tenants have little incentive to maintain and protect their building and grounds from damage. Landlords lose the incentive to make repairs and installations when they cannot recover those expenses from rental receipts. But raising rents either arouses the ire of tenants or forces them to move. Too many move and the landlord is forced to abandon his property, since buyers of rental buildings are hard to come by these days. Tenants say that landlords are making plenty by taking advantage of tax breaks and other concessions. Some of them, probably most of them, are. But then there are others who are walking away from their buildings. The problem is so complex that the situation has no easy answers. Housing experts have yet to come up with broad, acceptable proposals that would halt abandonment and yet make for a better equality between the renter, who always gets short shrift, and the building owner who, whatever his problems, is still the "lord of the land." Gains *are* being made to help the former. The courts have begun to realize that landlord–tenant law is poorly adapted to the needs of tenants and have been making landmark, albeit regional, decisions in their favor. Tenants in some instances can now sue the landlord where such a suit would once have been grounds for termination of lease. Landlords' nonresponsibility for on-premises accidents and robberies is being hacked away at. Retaliatory evictions are being halted. Legislators are suffering through consciousness-raising sessions of their own—awakening to (if nothing else) the realization of the enormous bloc of votes represented by renters. They have introduced and passed many tenant-oriented bills. The newest one slowly wafting across the country allows income tax deductions to renters similar to homeowners' mortgage interest and property tax allowances. Almost all these changes and the even greater number of bills now in legislative hoppers are the result of persistent lobbying by tenants' groups. Landlords have always been organized into real estate associations, building owner associations, and similar fraternities. They have had lobbyists stationed in Washington and in state capitals to protect their interests. Now building tenant unions and regional coalitions have banded together to press their needs in the same manner.

But this book does not mainly concern itself with theories about, and suggestions for improving, the landlord–tenant imbroglio. Rather it is written for renters, to answer their questions on the day-to-day problems of vertical living, an area that has heretofore been largely overlooked in the mass preoccupation with single-family homeowning. Covered in this book are the minutiae that probably occupy the mind and time of tenants far more than amorphous musings on the rental condition. Questions such as "What can I do about the leak in the bathroom ceiling?" "Which door locks are best?" "When is a doorman tipped, and how much?" "Should I buy theft insurance?" "Are those *cockroaches?!!*" For the tenant who wants to combine apartment living with ownership benefits, the advantages of the cooperative and condominium housing styles are discussed. Those who prefer renting will find a guide to apartment hunting.

However, woven in the next few hundred pages are sometimes not-so-subtle messages to get the tenant moving toward change.

Information on how to nudge the landlord in order to get what is due, to keep after city agencies, to try the courts, to form a tenant organization or join one, to lobby for stronger legislation. The power of numbers cannot be argued, but change can also start with determined individuals dealing with their housing problems in smaller arenas. One tenant and his landlord. One tenant before a judge.

Little strokes . . .

CHAPTER 2

□

Apartment Hunting

Looking for an apartment is a little less traumatic than house hunting. There is, after all, no need for a renter to be concerned about such items as chimney cracks, puddles in the basement, or the ominous-sounding "dry rot." Nor will he have to burden himself with a $20,000 or more mortgage for the better part of the rest of his life.

But if the responsibility of ownership is missing, a tenant can still find plenty in the rental process to stew over. He may be looking for an apartment in a community where there are few vacancies. He may have to move from his present building in a hurry if, for example, it is being demolished or he has been evicted. He may also run into discriminatory (sex, marital status, and so forth) rent practices. Rents increase steadily, while the amount of mortgage payments is fixed. And the apartment finally chosen had better be in good condition because it is often difficult to get repairs made by a surly landlord. Or the superintendent. Or a handyman.

Getting organized

If a little time can be spared, it should be spent collecting your thoughts before starting out to look. What do you want in an apartment? What can't you do without? And what will you settle for?

Rent, of course, is the foremost consideration. How high can you go without strapping yourself? One-quarter of a month's salary is a good guideline, but if a nice place to live is worth sacrificing in other areas, you may feel you can go higher. For renters in the $20,000-plus income bracket, a wiser move might be investment in a condominium or cooperative to take advantage of the tax breaks and equity buildup that go with ownership.

Location is also important. Your rent ceiling will dictate to some extent where you will look. Which of those suitable areas is more convenient? Commuting to work may be longer at the new address, or it may be the same distance but now you will have to crisscross town on two buses (at two fares) instead of one. If you must be close to a school, that is another important consideration, for many people these days choose their homes from those situated in the better school districts. How far away are churches, synagogues, stores or shopping centers? A quiet residential street may sound like bliss to a rattled inner-city dweller, but without a car how will you haul groceries from the supermarket eight blocks away?

Then consider the complexion of the building in which you are interested. Most people prefer to live among their peers, which accounts, in part, for the success of singles only and all-adult and retirement communities. Alvin Toffler in his book *Future Shock* says that improved technology is making a wide variety of experiences and choices available and is giving man increasing opportunities to express his individuality. That is what the real estate industry is saying, too. They are aiming at narrower markets, at people who share specific characteristics or interests. For example, there is a development in Kalamazoo, Michigan,

that could be characterized as a community for nature lovers.
And Edward Havlik, president of Home Data, Inc., in Chicago,
believes we can soon look for developments for sports enthusiasts
and complexes for working parents that will include day care
centers. Sweden, always in the vanguard, already has this latter
type of complex, which they call "service houses." Besides the
usual amenities, these high-rise apartment buildings contain
all-day nurseries for children, a separate supervised playground
for them and—what may be the biggest boon of all for the
working couple—an inexpensive self-service restaurant for tenants in the building.

Apartment complexes for clearly defined lifestyles naturally
give a prospective tenant a good picture of life within. But in the
overwhelming majority of more anonymous buildings you should
take a look at the people you see in the lobby or on the grounds.
Are they predominantly senior citizens? Lots of young couples
with small children? Do you think you will fit in or stand out?

Throughout your search, be realistic. "Dream houses" may still
be found, but there is no such thing as the perfect apartment. The
rent may be more than you can comfortably afford, the floors
may be in bad shape, the building may be too noisy or it may be
located too far out of town. But it *is* important to like *something*
about the place you finally take. Even two years is too long a time
to spend in an apartment one hates.

What kind of building?

There are many styles to choose from. The following classifica-
tions may overlap a little, but in general rental housing units can
be easily recognized as:

ULTRA-LUXURY These are usually old, architecturally impressive buildings with very high rents. Construction of the
apartments is excellent: They have thick plaster walls to muffle
noise, 12–14 foot ceilings, and handsome lobbies with solid wood

furniture and fresh flowers instead of the laminate and plastic plants found in lesser imitations. The luxury building will also have a large service staff, all of whom expect to be tipped regularly—and well.

A word of caution: If you want to stay put a while after you move in, ask some of the tenants or call the housing reporter of your local newspaper to see if there have been rumors of the building going cooperative or condominium. Conversions are rampant these days, and the more prestigious rental properties are the first to switch.

MODERN HIGH-RISES   A notch or two below ultra-luxury level in construction and appointments (here is where you'll find the thin walls and plastic flora), but the rents are still high. Although their bland appearance is interchangeable from Washington, D.C. to Washington state, the buildings are generally satisfactory. Since the young singles set seems to gravitate to glossy high-rises, there can be a lot of traffic, an unusually high turnover rate, and frequent noisy parties.

TOWNHOUSES   A variable lot encompassing haughty mansions off Fifth Avenue in Manhattan to San Francisco's imaginatively colored Victorians. Although they were single-family dwellings at one time, many of them have since been divided into apartments. Rents depend on the condition of the house and its location, but in general they are high.

Townhouses can also be a form of condominium development. In that context they are usually new complexes consisting of groupings of two- or three-story attached houses.

GARDEN APARTMENTS   A unit with the entrance on the first floor and the use of a back or front yard or terrace. This can be the first floor of a brownstone, but more often the term refers to a development in a suburban or exurban setting with grass, trees and sometimes a swimming pool and tennis courts. A garden apartment can be expensive or not, but is almost always less costly than a high-rise building. Remember that the lower-rent garden communities seem to attract a large number of families with small children. Keep an eye out for baby carriages, tricycles, and other children's items on the lawn or in the vestibules to give you an idea of the makeup of the complex.

BROWNSTONES   Literally, a reddish-brown sandstone dwelling, but nowadays a generic term used to describe any row house at least fifty years old and constructed of stone. Brownstone renovation in urban centers is going full blast right now. If the apartment you are looking at is in a still undiscovered neighborhood you may turn up a real find, even if the setting is somewhat shabby. Brownstones are as good as, and often even better than, the highest-rent luxury building. Many feature stained glass windows, wooden shutters, corniced ceilings, marble fireplaces, wide-planked floors and other elegant touches of long-gone days. Another advantage to brownstone living is that the owner usually lives in the building and therefore the upkeep is good.

But if you're hunting in an enclave that appears to be in the midst of a renaissance, you are probably too late for low rent. Look what restoration did to rent scales in Brooklyn Heights, Washington's Georgetown and similar revival areas.

RENOVATED BUILDINGS   Nondescript apartment houses of six or so stories, usually walkups, that have been spruced up to command higher rents. But even with the price increase, rents are often well below luxury level—a good meat-and-potatoes buy. The apartments are usually quite clean, often with new appliances, and are in a fair neighborhood.

PUBLIC HOUSING   A term used to describe housing built and owned by a public agency for eligible low-income families. Also called "low-rent housing" or "municipal housing." Subsidized housing projects are administered by the local housing authority. Rents are set according to the income levels of the residents— usually $4,000 and below is considered low income—and there are strict requirements for admission. Unfortunately, in appearance the developments usually run the short gamut from institutional gloomy to bland. Information about public housing can be obtained from your local housing authority or from the U.S. Department of Housing and Urban Development (HUD), Washington, D.C. 20410. They will have the names, addresses, rents, and admission requirements of projects in your area.

RAILROAD APARTMENTS   Usually found in tenement buildings, these units are laid out so that one room follows another, railroad car style.

TENEMENTS   No need to describe the appearance of this type of housing, which is usually a block of five- or six-story stone or frame row houses in a rundown section of town. But if you can close your eyes to a dilapidated exterior, inside you may find an excellent bargain—large, airy rooms and several more of them than you would be able to afford in a better neighborhood.

Knuckling down

September and October are difficult months to hunt because students are settling down for the college year and people who waited until after summer to change jobs—and addresses—are also in the market for new housing. Also, many times leases run out in September. But aside from the early fall, no one time is better than another to find an apartment. Do try to avoid weekends, however, when everyone else is canvassing. If you can, do your looking during weekday hours or in the evenings.

Let everyone know you want an apartment—friends, relatives, co-workers, neighborhood merchants. Any one of them might set you on to the right place.

Walk through the sections of town you would consider moving into. This is also a way to see if you'll feel safe walking those streets at night. Doormen often know when there are vacancies in their buildings. Talk to some of them. Yes, in an area with low vacancy levels you will have to cross their palms. The amount can be $10 or $100 or even as much as one month's rent for a *tip* on a vacant apartment and the name and phone number of the managing agent. Sometimes you can find a vacant apartment by looking at accessible mailboxes and spotting one with no namecard. (Although you may have to do some investigating to determine whether the apartment is really vacant or if the namecard is merely missing.) Or a set of bare windows may give you a clue to a vacancy. In brownstone neighborhoods where the landlord usually lives in the building, it is easier still to inquire about vacancies while you're out walking.

Newspaper ads

The classified advertisements in the daily newspaper are an important aid to the apartment hunter. The large display ads tell a great deal about the buildings they are touting since they list rents and special features, sometimes down to the brand names of appliances. The classified ads, on the other hand, can be almost unintelligible. The reason for the constricted writing is that advertising rates often run as high as $7 a line, so economy in wording is essential, especially since many of the classified advertisers are small landlords with only one or two buildings to fill. That is why you will see a cryptic

riv vu, hi flr, so expos, quiet 5 rms 2 x-lg for dr or 3d br,
mod eat-in k, wbfp, 744-5880.

If the advertiser did not have to be concerned about cost, he would have been able to tell a prospective tenant that the apartment he is renting has a view of the river, is on a high floor in what must therefore be a relatively modern building. It is bright and sunny with the southern exposure dear to greenery. There are five quiet rooms (no doubt with good, sound walls), two of which are not tiny sewing or dressing rooms, but are large enough to be used for another bedroom or a dining room. There is a modern kitchen which will accommodate a dinette set. And there is a woodburning fireplace.

The telephone number at the end of the ad may mean that the landlord himself is doing the advertising. Or it may be the number of a broker. Management companies, who run apartment houses for the owners, usually list their names in classified ads. They charge no fee, while brokers do.

Here are how some other commonly used abbreviations translate:

A/C	Room air conditioner(s). You pay the electricity bill.
cen A/C	Central air conditioning. Usually provided at no extra charge.
cons	Concessions made by the landlord to stimulate renting. Can be one or two months' free rent. Or perhaps membership in the building's swimming club at no additional charge.
dup	Duplex. An apartment on two floors.
Floor thru	An apartment taking up an entire floor, usually in a brownstone or other building that was once a single-family residence.
frplc	Fireplace. But it's usually there just for adornment unless the ad reads "working frplc" or "wbfp"—woodburning fireplace.
Society Hill area; Pacific Heights area	The key word is "area." An advertising come-on usually meaning the apartment is on the *fringe* of a desirable neighborhood. How good it is depends on the condition of the streets ringing those more fashionable addresses.

Sometimes, too, brokers use this heading when they have a number of buildings for rent in the same section of town.

lanai A Hawaiian word for balcony.

L or L-shaped A living area in the shape of the letter L. The bottom line of the L is often used for a dining area or, in a studio apartment, for a sleeping area.

lux Luxury, a euphemism for high rent.

pull k Pullman kitchen. The stove, sink and refrigerator are lined up along one wall, but not enclosed in a separate room.

sec Depends on the advertiser's interpretation. Could mean security deposit is required, but more often tells the apartment hunter the building has good, or at least adequate, protective devices.

The size of an apartment listed in an advertisement can also be a puzzlement. What is considered a room? Is a bathroom a full room or the demi "½"? Opinions vary, but generally bathrooms, foyers, alcoves, dinettes, kitchenettes and terraces are not considered full rooms. The area must usually have at least one window and a minimum floor area of fifty square feet or so to be called a room. Landlords sometimes raise room counts to get higher rents. A "nook" suddenly becomes a whole room. Sometimes one long room will be counted as two. A studio is transformed into a three-room apartment, which of course it is if you count the bathroom and kitchenette as full rooms. Throw in a walk-in closet and why not call it a four-room apartment? An on-site inspection of any apartment will tell you what's being gotten away with here, but classified ads can be misleading. Clarify the actual space to your satisfaction before traipsing off to see any promising place.

To give you some idea of room count, here is how the Real Estate Board of New York, Inc., defines living areas:

Description of Unit	Room Count
Living room, bath, wall kitchenette	1 room
Living room, bath, walk-in kitchenette	1½ rooms
Living room, bath, walk-in kitchenette plus dining alcove or dining foyer	2 rooms
Living room, bath, walk-in kitchenette plus dining alcove or dining foyer and sleeping alcove	2½ rooms
Living room, bedroom, bath, walk-in kitchenette	2½ rooms
Living room, bedroom, bath, walk-in kitchenette plus dining alcove or dining foyer	3 rooms
Living room, bedroom, bath, full kitchen plus dining alcove or dining foyer	3½ rooms
Living room, 2 bedrooms, bath, walk-in kitchenette plus dining alcove or dining foyer	4 rooms
Living room, 2 bedrooms, bath, full kitchen plus dining alcove or dining foyer	4½ rooms
Living room, 2 bedrooms, bath, dining room, full kitchen	5 rooms

Sunday is usually the best day for classified advertisements. If you purchase early copies of the paper you may beat out your competition for the choicer (low-rent) apartments. The circulation department of your area newspaper can tell you where in town the first editions are delivered.

You might consider running your own classified ad under "Apartments Wanted." Sometimes landlords look first to that column to save themselves money, time, and the irritation of showing hordes of prospects through their properties. If what you are renting or seeking to rent is very prestigious (translation: high-rent) or if you are having trouble finding a sublet, classified advertisements in the back of such magazines as *New York, Saturday Review/World, Harper's* and *Atlantic* afford excellent additional exposure.

Brokers

Real estate brokers charge fees of one month's rent or a portion, usually 10 percent, of the annual rent to find an apartment. Register with several, but be careful about signing anything until *after* they have found an apartment for you. You should not have to pay anything *before*. Brokers can, of course, be very helpful, but do try to get as many details about an apartment as you can before going out to see it. "Yeah, yeah there's a view of the river," may turn out to be a peek at the water from the upper right hand corner of the bathroom window. And unless the broker has personally visited the building he cannot be expected to know if the neighborhood is clean or if the streets appear safe.

Other ploys

Probably every comedian's joke file contains the old chestnut about the desperate tenant scouring the obituary notices for the latest vacant apartment. Finding one, he hurries to the building to discover that the deceased's physician has just rented it. Well, it's true that if newspaper ads and brokers produce no results, the apartment hunter will have to become more inventive.

One young couple planning to be married printed flyers announcing their need for an apartment and left them in the mailboxes at several buildings in the neighborhood they wanted. They distributed 200 sheets. It was an offbeat idea, and it would be nice to be able to report that they found a plum of an apartment. But they didn't. In fact, they got nary a nibble. What *could* work, however, is if that same request were typed on an index card and pinned on bulletin boards in nearby churches, stores, and especially in colleges with their transient populations. In an area where there are large corporations, ask if you can run a classified ad for an apartment in their house organs.

Getting back to the newspapers, look at the Sunday real estate *news* section before flipping back to the classifieds. When a company is reported leaving town the employees who choose to go along will be leaving apartments behind. Perhaps the firm will allow you to put an "Apartment Wanted" card on their bulletin board.

"Key money"

If the previous tenant has made extensive—and expensive—repairs or installations in an apartment, he may try to get back some of his money by charging several hundred or even thousands of dollars in addition to the rent to make the apartment available. In other instances he may want to dispose of unwanted pieces of furniture and make a little profit besides, so he puts a price tag on them. If you want the apartment, you must pay the additional money. Usually the request is made by the tenant before he notifies the landlord of his intention to move. You pay him what he asks and then he informs the landlord he is moving and has found a suitable replacement. This is an occasional, not frequent, practice in cities with a desperately low apartment vacancy rate. The apartments are often in tenement buildings or are lofts. Landlords also sometimes extract a hefty sum from prospective renters in return for leasing a rent-controlled apartment. Although galling to the apartment hunter, "key money" is not illegal.

Apartment finding services

Not to be confused with legitimate brokers, these businesses have sprung up only recently and are giving enormous headaches to regulatory agencies. The services charge a flat $25 to $35 to find an apartment for a client. The money is payable in advance, a demand no legitimate broker should make for finding an apartment and one no tenant should consider. The firms, sometimes called "apartment locating agencies," hand the apartment hunter a list of available units in town. But the listings are often fictitious, or taken straight from local classified advertisements, or are composed of apartments that are already occupied.

If you are going to use any agency to help you find an apartment, check them out first with your Better Business Bureau and/or Department of State. And find out from the agency precisely what they are guaranteeing for your money.

Roommate placement agencies

Rare is the single apartment dweller who has not at one time or another had a roommate. If you would rather move into an already established setup, or if you have an apartment and are looking for someone to share the rent, you might look into roommate placement agencies. They are a relatively new enterprise established for the express purpose of bringing apartment sharers together. They can be a much easier and more pleasant way to find a roommate than combing the "Apartments to Share" classifieds.

Few of the services are more than five years old, but almost all major cities now have at least one, and in the larger metropolitan areas there are often several agencies to choose from.

The firms are not yet regulated by most city or state bureaus, but despite the lack of supervision they appear to be well run, unlike the apartment finding firms. There have been almost no complaints registered against roommate agencies at Better Business Bureaus or consumer affairs organizations.

The agencies say that, like marriage, a successful roommate situation is based on both parties having pretty much the same background and interests. No odd couples, please. Applicants are usually presented with questionnaires designed to ferret out personality traits and lifestyles. Although the questionnaires start with the usual age, education, and line of work queries, they then become more probing. Do you generally go to bed before midnight or are you a night person? Are you tidy, average or very sloppy? Do you want a roommate who will become a close friend or would you prefer someone who will merely share the rent? How do you feel about drugs?

When the questionnaires have been checked over—and at some firms this is done by computer—people who should be compatible are put in touch with each other.

Agencies guarantee applicants as many referrals as it takes to make a match. After all, there's somebody for everybody. So one can keep looking through an agency's card file until every likely prospect is exhausted.

If you have an apartment and are looking for someone to share, some firms will ask to see it and will—chilling thought—rate its assets and drawbacks. For instance they may tell applicants your apartment is on a high floor in a luxury building, but that it is sparsely furnished. Or the rent includes utilities, but the building is not air conditioned. They will even list the appliances you have. That way the potential roommate who comes knocking on your door will at least have some idea of what waits within.

As might be expected, young, single adults form the bulk of roommate agencies' clientele. But doubling up is not limited to the post-college group. Also seeking to fight high rents, or sometimes just plain loneliness, are a growing number of older people, particularly women in their fifties and sixties. And, a product of skyrocketing divorce rates, many formerly married women with small children. Most services will handle these more difficult placements, but the match will take longer than one involving the more plentiful singles.

Despite today's casual living arrangements, all agencies place only men with men and women with women. They won't even listen to requests for coed sharers. Some agencies shy away from placing homosexuals, but others find them lucrative—they say the turnover rate is high.

Applications must be made in person: You can't phone in a request. Fees vary, of course, but generally they run from $15 to $40, depending on whether one is looking for an apartment or already has one and is looking for a sharer. In the latter case the rate is lower. Sometimes that one fee is good for a replacement during the year if the first match didn't work out. But usually it's one roommate for one fee. Of course, if the arrangement turns out to be a disaster after only a few days you're entitled to another selection.

The favorite choice of the young career set? Airline stewardesses and traveling salesmen—they aren't around much!

Discriminatory practices in renting

It is against the law to discriminate in renting on the basis of race, creed, color or national origin. In a very, very few states and municipalities it is also against the law to reject prospective renters on the basis of sex. Single women, formerly married women with or without children, and unmarried mothers often find it enormously difficult—and in some cases impossible—to find an apartment, regardless of their financial background and employment record. New York City and New York State have effective legislation barring discrimination on the basis of sex, but other areas of the country show little interest in enacting similar laws. Enactment of the Equal Rights Amendment will wipe out this type of discrimination.

Discrimination on any basis can take several forms. The landlord can refuse outright to show or rent an apartment, or he can enormously inflate the rent. An extra month's security or additional money for services that are known to be free to other residents can be charged.

If you feel you have been discriminated against: 1) have someone you feel would have no trouble getting the apartment apply for it. But his or her job, income, length of employment, former residence and references should be similar to yours so that you will be able to prove later that you were turned down solely because of your race, creed, etc.; 2) check with your local human rights commission. The bureaus' exact titles differ from one state to another. Look for the words "Fair Practices" or "Human Relations" in their titles. If your rights *have* been violated, those offices will try to work out the problem and get you the apartment you are entitled to. You might also see a lawyer with the thought of suing the landlord. If you win the case you will almost certainly win the apartment—and money damages as well. Once you are in the apartment, harassment will cease. In a large complex the owners will forget about you. The landlord of a small building will never be exactly friendly, but then how many tenants and landlords are?

What to look for in an apartment

Probably the most important overall advice for the would-be tenant once he starts going through apartments is to have any repairs or installations that he wants made written into the lease before signing it. The landlord or agent showing you through an apartment may orally agree to fix any number of things in order to get you to sign, or to speed up the inspection tour or just to be pleasant. But try to hold them to their promises after you have moved in! If it's there in writing, you stand a better chance. On the lease you should write in ink any promises the landlord makes, initial the additions and then have him initial them. Initial each item separately, even if there are fifteen different ones. Any defects in the apartment—worn spots on the rugs, chipped walls, etc.—should also be noted in the lease, and even photographed by you, so they will not be attributed to you at moving time and will not hold up the return of your security deposit.

Another smart move would be to talk to one or two of the residents of the building. You can stop them in the lobby, or get their names from the mailboxes and follow up with a phone call. Or, if you have access to one, you can look up their names and phone numbers in a reverse telephone directory that lists subscribers by address rather than by name.

Ask the tenants questions you can be sure a landlord is not

going to answer gladly. Such as whether the building has a cockroach problem. Or whether there has been talk of its going co-op or condominium. Find out if there is a tenant group and if so, why did they organize? You might also inquire if requests for repairs are answered promptly. Maybe the building has a newsletter, and the tenant you're questioning would send you a copy to give you an idea of the composition of the tenantry, their activities, and so on. The newsletter will give you a good idea of their gripes about building services, too.

Other important points to consider on your inspections:

RENT Naturally your first question about any apartment will be "how much?" At some point in your apartment hunt, especially if you are moving to a new city or state and are not familiar with rent patterns or regulations there, check with the local housing or rent office for rent guidelines in the area. You should know, for example, if rents are wide open, or if there is a freeze on them, or if there is a rent control statute, limiting the amount a landlord can raise the rent in a new apartment.

Can you bargain for a lower rent? Not in a seller's market. But if the apartment needs a good deal of work which you'll gladly do yourself, then you may win a rent reduction.

COMPLAINTS Ask who is the on-premises supervisor of the building. He may be called a superintendent or a janitor or a resident manager or he may be a part-time worker who oversees a number of buildings on the block. What can he be expected to do in the line of making repairs, accepting rent checks, taking in packages, etc.?

DOORMEN Opinions vary on the worth of a doorman, although his presence does lend a certain air of dignity to a building. Doormen are either excellent or terrible, with no rating in between. A good doorman knows his tenants by sight and greets them. He calls cabs for them, takes in parcels and is a reassuring sight in the 2 A.M. lobby. But too many doormen are at the opposite end of the quality scale. Their uniforms look shabby or they do not know tenants from visitors. They allow dry cleaners and other neighborhood deliverymen access to an apartment rather than going up with them or accepting the package and holding it downstairs for the tenant's return. And they never seem to be around when you want them. You should be able to tell which category your prospective doorman falls into by observing him a short time and chatting with him briefly.

FLOOR PLAN   Check the overall layout of the apartment. A beautifully designed floor plan isn't vital, but an apartment shouldn't be obviously awkward. Can you, for instance, see into the bathroom from the doorway? Do you step right into the kitchen? Bring along a tape measure to measure doorways and walls to be sure they can accommodate large or unusually shaped pieces of furniture.

VIEW   Rents generally increase about $10–15 a floor the higher you go in a luxury building. Plant lovers will naturally check the layout for light and exposure.

UTILITIES   Are they included in the rent or must you pay the electric and gas bill yourself?

HEAT AND AIR   If you're hunting in the summer, it will be hard to tell how the building's heating system works, unless you talk to one of the tenants. Thermostats or radiators in each apartment are, of course, far more desirable than a master system where the tenants have no control over the temperature in their individual units.

Ask if the building has central air conditioners or room air conditioners or no air conditioners. Some older structures are not wired for air conditioning, or have odd-sized windows that will not accommodate room coolers. If you take such an apartment, you will have to be prepared to swelter through the summers with only a fan for comfort.

NOISE   Unfortunately, this form of pollution seems to go along with apartment life. Quite a few jokes from the old card file here too, such as overhearing the arguments of the couple next door or the cacophony of flushing toilets or the tap-dancing on the bare floor upstairs (although most leases specify that a certain percentage of bare floor area *must* be covered). In an older, well-constructed building you may have solid plaster walls which help mute noise. But in newer buildings they will more likely be a flimsy dry-wall construction, through which you can almost hear a dripping faucet. When looking at an apartment send someone into the next room and see how loudly he has to talk before being heard where you are.

First floor apartments are, surprisingly, often quieter than those higher up because the trees and shrubbery tend to muffle sound. Don't go too far down, however. Basement apartments get more than their share of water bugs!

Carpeting and heavy draperies and even wall hangings will help absorb unwanted sounds. If there are gaps around the windows and doors, try weather stripping. A self-adhesive foam stripping is inexpensive and will keep out the weather as well as street noise.

Noise can also come from a railroad near the apartment you are considering, or a fire station or even a school. If you work during the day, lunchtime and dismissal racket won't bother you. But what if you are home then? And what about summer evenings when the playground is open late to the youngsters?

Take a good look at the buildings ringing your prospective apartment, too. Is there a vacant lot where a high-rise is soon to go up? More noise, guaranteed for at least a year.

KITCHEN   Tenants moving from private homes into apartments for the first time are especially appalled at the size of apartment kitchens. The rest of us have grown used to it. If we are not shown a pullman unit, then it is often a seven-by-ten-foot "tunnel kitchen" with about one and a half square feet of counter space. Only in older buildings, luxury or tenement, do there seem to be kitchens roomy enough to eat in.

Turn on the kitchen light and take a fast look around to see if there are any cockroaches. If you do see one or two, ask if extermination is provided regularly and at no charge to tenants.

Check the overall condition of the appliances. If there is no window in the room, there should be a wall fan or an overhead hood on the stove with an updraft pull.

BATHROOM   Try all the fixtures to make sure everything works. Here again, if there is no window, there should be a wall fan. Look for a broken or missing toilet paper spindle and for a badly chipped soap dish or toothbrush holder. Porcelain and ceramic tile *can* be repaired. Yellowish or brown stains around pipes indicate a leak. If the room is wall-to-wall contact paper, run your hand over it. It may be concealing crumbling or cracked plaster. Actually it is a good idea to be suspicious of any surface covered with contact paper or simulated bricks or any other similar covering that can conceal a multitude of structural sins.

ELECTRICAL OUTLETS   Be sure there are plenty. One couple had to run an extension cord under the living room rug clear to the other side of the room to hook up with the only outlet.

GARBAGE   Ask if there is an incinerator or if you have to haul the garbage downstairs yourself to a utility room. Glance into the incinerator closet. If it's messy, you have an idea of the housekeeping habits of your future neighbors—and of the quality of maintenance in the building.

CLOSET SPACE   There is never enough.

STORAGE   Few small buildings can provide for tenants' trunks and cartons, but the larger ones do have storage room in the basement. Ask about a place to park bicycles.

LAUNDRY   Is there a laundry room on the premises? If not, find out if there is a laundromat nearby.

PARKING   Even though the building has a parking lot, there may be no room for your car. Ask how parking spots are allotted, if one will be available for your car and if there is a monthly charge.

TELEVISION   Is there a master antenna on the roof with which you can hook up? Is the building wired for cable television? Has the landlord already turned thumbs down on cable TV?

AMENITIES   If the building is at all luxurious, do find out if there is a rooftop garden, swimming pool, sauna or game room. Surprisingly, some tenants never do discover the little extras their buildings have to offer. This is especially true of sublets and changing roommates who are not given the guided tour accorded the initial tenant. One man discovered, after living in his apartment for one year, that there was a tar beach on his roof complete with potted plants, deck chairs, and occasional parties. He overheard a conversation about the spot on the elevator.

Those niceties may not be free to tenants, though. Sometimes there is a membership fee or a one-time admission charge.

MAIL   Every tenant is entitled to his own mailbox, which is usually located in the lobby or the vestibule. But on the days when the mail runneth over, will the super or doorman take in the excess for you? What happens to parcel post packages and department store deliveries? Is it necessary to miss a morning's work to sit around and wait for a furniture delivery, or will the building staff admit the deliverymen?

SECURITY   See Chapter 6, "Security." But for a fast once-over on your inspection, ask if there are any special security devices in the building. In an apartment house with no doorman and an outside front door, that door should be kept locked with keys distributed to tenants. Apartments with skylights are lovely but great invitations to burglary. Other good news/bad news: A place fortified by gates on the windows, a special bolt on the door and a floor-to-door police lock is at first thought reassuring. But how many times must it have been ransacked for the previous tenant to have been driven to such elaborate precautions?

It's over; you have found the apartment. Not exactly what you wanted, but then this is an imperfect world. If the longed-for fireplace is missing, well, what about the unexpected delight of floor-to-ceiling windows? Truth to tell, the building is colorless. But the street—ah, one of the best in town. You are satisfied.

Next to consider: the lease.

CHAPTER 3

☐

The Lease

In an age of future shock, planned obsolescence, and other effects of our throwaway culture, the lease is a peculiar anachronism. Dating back to feudal times, when the "lord of the land" had all the rights and the vassals living on his property had none, the document has remained virtually unchanged to the present time.

There are hundreds of varieties of the standard residential lease now in effect across the country. There are special forms for furnished apartments, for rent-controlled apartments, for cooperatives. What they all have in common, besides minuscule print and archaic, almost impossible-to-read language, is the assignment of most rights to the landlord, perhaps one or two to the tenant. If he pays his rent on time and makes no trouble, he can stay.

But then why wouldn't the lease be so one-sided? Despite an impartial-sounding name in the corner of the documents, they are all drawn up by real estate boards or landlords' attorneys or legal-form stationery stores. Tenant groups have been fighting, with limited success, for reform of the standard lease in order to bring a better balance between the two parties. Revisions have also been suggested by the American Bar Foundation and in the Uniform Residential Landlord and Tenant Act, which was drafted by the National Conference of Commissioners on Uniform State Laws and is meeting with some success nationally. In the public housing area, with its more than 3 million tenants, lease revisions are being implemented by the U.S. Department of Housing and Urban Development.

However, substantive changes are coming very slowly. Some of the more easily made—and publicized—alterations are merely cosmetic, such as larger, more modern type faces and simpler language. Blumberg's, a stationery store in Manhattan that could be considered the department store of leases, supplying more than 5 million forms a year to New York, New Jersey, and Connecticut property owners, is constantly seeking revision of its many varieties of leases. But only to make them more understandable.

Landlords are understandably loath to change a document so heavily weighted in their favor. But orchids must go to one of them: The Kassuba Corporation, which operates 40,000 rental apartments across the country and which, in 1971, introduced a lease containing only ten paragraphs and a list of only twelve regulations (compared to twenty-four and twenty-six in some New York leases). Besides being relatively short, the lease is unusual in that it provides that the tenant may cancel the rental agreement on ninety days' notice—no waiting for its expiration. It also makes no provision that the tenant must waive trial by jury in the event of a conflict with the landlord, a standard clause in most other leases.

Leases, agreements and the spoken word

Some tenants never see a lease. At the time they agree to take an apartment the owner presents them with a "rental agreement" or the arrangement may be made orally.

A written agreement is somewhat less structured and shorter than the standard lease, often permitting month-to-month tenancy. It also allows the landlord to write in his own special preferences for how the tenant should conduct himself. And he can raise the rent whenever he wants during the run of the agreement, whereas with a lease the rent is fixed for the duration.

An oral agreement is just what it says, a spoken arrangement between landlord and tenant about the terms of the rental arrangement.

Which of the three is preferable? If you do not plan to stay the length of a typical lease—one, two or even three years—the rental or oral agreement would be best, although you should realize you are sacrificing some of the protection a lease offers—against a rent rise, for instance.

Remember too, the longer you stay under an oral agreement the more difficult it becomes for both sides to remember exactly what agreements were reached, an especially important point if you should end up in court because the landlord "forgot" an initial promise.

If you do plan to stay awhile and if you're in an area with a tight rental market, sign the lease. Slanted as it is, a lease does offer some protection against the vagaries of the rental system. If you are worried about being forced to move before its expiration, you might ask the landlord to write in a "transfer clause" that would let you out of the agreement if need be. Some leases contain similar "military clauses" for service people. Others, especially in university towns, have special nine-month terms for students.

Reading the lease

You do not need a lawyer to read over the lease for you. It just looks that way. For the most part, there is little the tenant can do but accept its terms or move on. Some people never bother reading the document at all before signing. Be a little smarter than that though. At least look over the parts that are typed in. And look for paragraphs that might spell trouble later on. If you have a pet, see what the lease says. If you plan to use your apartment for semi-professional purposes, look that up too. See if there is a sublet clause if you think you may be needing one. Don't be afraid to ask the landlord to change the wording of certain clauses or to add riders at the end of the document clarifying some point or making an exception to one of the covenants. About the pet, for instance: If the lease says no and the landlord says all right, have the change put in writing and initialed and dated by him. (Note first that in some cities pets are permitted by law.)

Adding to the lease repairs you want made is especially important. A man considering a fourth floor walkup one May morning was assured by his prospective landlord that the hole in the living room wall would soon be filled in by an air conditioner. The young man pleasantly agreed, and then he had the landlord add a sentence to the lease that an air conditioner was to be installed in just that space by June 1. Don't minimize the importance of having the slightest change you want made put in writing before you sign. Spoken promises can evaporate before the lease is back in the landlord's pocket. If yours is an oral agreement, those terms are legal and enforceable, but your case would be much more effective, should it ever come to court, if potentially troublesome points are put in writing.

Never sign a blank lease. Once you have signed, you should receive a copy of the document for your files.

Who signs the lease?

Landlords have the right by law to know how many people will be living in each apartment unit. Too many people is often a violation of the law but, as conditions in overcrowded ghetto buildings will attest, this is one clause that is often overlooked in lower income dwellings. Giving the landlord a nose count is no problem for a single person or a couple or a family, but for other apartment dwellers it may be.

The image portraying young career people spilling into the big cities and crowding themselves into tiny apartments with many and ever-changing roommates is true. Ask any secretary or accountant or other upwardly mobile type whose "bedroom" is the living room sofa. However, when bunches of roommates go apartment hunting it is best for just one or two persons who are willing to assume responsibility to sign the lease for, say, a $3\frac{1}{2}$-room, one-bedroom apartment. Landlords won't permit too many names on the lease for small quarters, but once the lease is signed, they generally leave you alone, that is, as long as the rent check comes in each month from a recognizable name. If the lease *specifically forbids additional tenants* besides the signer(s), taking another roommate or long-term guest could qualify you for eviction. If a signer moves out, a non-signer can apply for a new lease, but he or she will be treated as any new tenant and will be subject to a rent increase if one is scheduled for that apartment.

The case of a couple living together without the benefit of clergy, as the saying used to go, is also tricky. When one moves in with the other, well, the landlord often never knows or can't be bothered investigating. But when the couple goes apartment hunting together, there may be a problem. Cohabitation is against the law in some states. Even if it weren't, many landlords would refuse to rent to unmarried couples. It is best for one of the parties to sign the lease alone. Even when both names go up on the mailbox there may be harassment and eviction threats from the landlord. Keep reading the newspapers: A landmark court decision on this point is bound to come up soon.

One Philadelphia couple ran into an accommodating landlord who would rent them an apartment if they signed the lease "Mr. & Mrs.," even though they were not married. They signed and then worried. No need to, however. A couple living together today are merely two unmarried people living together—not common-law partners with all the obligations attendant on that status.

Security deposit

New tenants are almost always required to pay an additional sum of money over and above the first month's rent as "security" against possible damage, breakage or outright destruction of the premises by a careless tenant. Or against his skipping in the middle of the lease. The money is supposed to be returned to the tenant when he moves out, leaving the apartment in satisfactory condition. This is a fair requirement: Property owners have a right to protect their investments.

But as sound as it is in theory, the security deposit in practice is the cause of more confusion, anger, and court cases than any other area of the rental relationship.

Landlords should specify just what they mean by "security" and especially whether it will be refunded. Sometimes the money is not called a security deposit at all, further adding to the confusion. If your landlord is asking for a "fee," it is probably nonreturnable. If it is called a "deposit" it should be, as the word implies, money you will see again. By its wording in the lease, you should be able to see whether the amount can be charged to "damages," "rent," or "repairs," none of which should be applicable to other areas, such as:

CLEANING FEE   This provides for cleaning of the apartment either before the tenant moves in or after he leaves. A $25 or so charge, it is nonreturnable.

ADVANCE RENT   This is simply an extra month's rent, usually applicable to the last month in residence. But ask to be sure.

LAST MONTH'S RENT   It is just what it says. When you give the landlord thirty days' notice of your intent to move, the last month's rent you paid at lease-signing will cover the remainder of your stay. This is not a security deposit, however, and cannot be used by the landlord to pay for damages. If he wants to do that and you have paid no security money that can be attached, he will have to sue. Actually, if you have a choice between the last month's rent or a security deposit, take the rent. It is money you will have to pay anyway, and you are spared the hassle of trying to get the other back.

SECURITY DEPOSIT Aha. As small claims courts, Better Business Bureaus, tenant unions, and arbitrators can attest, the overwhelming number of cases they handle are tenants trying to get back security money from a landlord who won't let go of it. The landlord's action is understandable when you consider that those dollars are tax free and are accumulating interest for him. Granted there are renters who leave the place in shambles, and those who walk out on $3\frac{1}{2}$ rooms lacquered a royal blue. They deserve to leave all or part of the money behind. Referring to tenant abuse of apartments, the general manager of one 2,000-plus unit complex in the Midwest said he found three out of ten departing tenants leave their units damaged in some way. "There is often a fine line between normal wear and tear and definite damage to the premises and furnishings," he said. "We always try to give the renter the benefit of the doubt. But a smashed door or a half dozen cigarette burns in the carpet do not constitute normal wear."

That's all true enough. But in many, many more cases tenants do leave the premises in good shape, but recalcitrant landlords have to be dragged into court to return the money. A couple of years ago *Apartment Life* magazine studied a 1,200-unit development in San Francisco that had a reputation for almost never returning security deposits. That habit added about $60,000 a year to the project's profit, the magazine calculated. More recently, a spokesman for the San Francisco Bay Area Tenants Action Project says the number of cases there in which the landlord will not return the security deposit is increasing each month. "Most of the time he doesn't give a reason or gives an invalid reason," the project stated.

Few states have laws spelling out tenant rights regarding security deposits, which is no doubt why so many battles over the money are brought to court. Most of the claims fall into three categories:

1) You are justly entitled to a full rebate of a month's rent since your lease has expired, you have notified the landlord of your intention to move *in writing* (orally won't hold up in court), and you are leaving the place in mint condition, or at least as good as you found it. The landlord is just being ornery about sending you the check. If you find yourself in this position, bring along with you to court any pictures of the apartment you took before you moved in (see "Apartment Hunting")—the overall shots, close-ups of defective wall areas, worn spots on the rug if the apartment was furnished, etc. And pictures of how the place looked when you left. If you've rented a floor waxer or a rug shampooer, hold on to the receipts and bring a picture of you using them. They will all strengthen your case. The court also advises you to bring along any witnesses who might help your cause. If they cannot or will not appear in person, take their written statements.

2) You are leaving before the lease expires, but are still claiming a refund. Douglas Matthews in his book *Sue the B*st*rds*, a consumer guide to small claims court, has found that many leases contain clauses whereby if a tenant leaves after six months or so he must pay a fee equal to one month's rent for the inconvenience caused the landlord in re-renting. But Mr. Matthews, who is a lawyer, claims that even tenants caught in such a lease can use Small Claims Court to get one-half or all that security money back if theirs is an apartment-short urban area where the landlord will have no trouble finding another tenant. Mr. Matthews suggests that you notify the landlord by mail of your intention to leave, and give at least one month's notice. Offer to find someone to take over the rest of your lease. The landlord will probably say no to that since he no doubt intends to raise the rent and would rather find a new tenant himself. But the

advantage to that strategy is that when you get to court you can tell the judge that you have been unreasonably refused permission to sublet. There was no need for the landlord to be left in the lurch, since you knew some nice folks willing to sublet.

If you are leaving because the landlord refuses to fix something that is seriously wrong with the apartment, that is a lawsuit of another color. Better consult your tenant group or a lawyer. You may have a full-fledged court case here, with a possible collection on moving and other related expenses that would go well over the $500 maximum claim of Small Claims Court.

3) You have paid an agent or landlord for holding the apartment for you for a specified length of time and now you've changed your mind. In most cases you're probably out of luck unless, for example, the landlord promised to make certain repairs on the apartment before you moved in and then didn't, or you're in an area where a vacant apartment is snapped up quickly. Then you *might* stand a chance of getting at least part of your money back. You pays your court fee and takes your chances.

This is a good place to mention the most common ruse of tenants trying to get back a security deposit: Withholding the last month's rent to make sure they will have no refund hassle when it comes time to move. Tenants leaving an area, knowing they will have no chance to get to Small Claims Court, merely notify the landlord that in lieu of the last month's rent they will apply the deposit rebate. He won't be pleased, but he will figure by the time he gets into court the tenant will have left town—and presumably left the apartment in good condition. But this strategy can be tricky. Leave too much notice and a landlord *will* have time to start eviction proceedings and perhaps get results. Rent withholding—for any reason—is grounds for eviction.

Not all problems with security deposits concern getting the money back. Tenants have other gripes:

1) Many landlords demand not just one month's extra rent, but sometimes two or even three months'. Occasionally the total amount of a security deposit is a flat $35 or $50, but usually it is based on the monthly rent. So, rents being what they are these days, the middle-income signer of a lease for a $175 apartment found through a broker could conceivably be forking over $875 before even moving in.

What can be done? Very little. Only a handful of states have laws regulating security deposits. Only two—Arizona and Washington—have at this writing passed laws based on the Uniform Residential Landlord and Tenant Act. A suggested limitation of one month's rent as security is one clause in that code.

2) Another gripe is receiving no interest on the security money when it is handed back after two, three or more years.   What can be done? Thanks to tenants' lobbying efforts, in a growing number of communities security deposits must now be placed in special accounts with interest at the prevailing rates paid to tenants. The landlord may deduct 1 percent for administrative costs. Tenants must be notified in which bank the deposit has been made, and interest is to be paid annually or held in trust until the expiration of the lease. The exact terms of the ruling vary. In New Jersey, for instance, where the "tenant security bill" was signed in 1973, if the landlord does not supply the name and address of the bank within thirty days after receiving the security deposit, the tenant is permitted to use the money toward his rent.

If your money is not returned two weeks after your departure, and the owner does not answer phone calls or letters, you're going to be in for a hard time in getting the money back. Better seek outside help.

Rent

Rent is due the first day of each month. In a small building you can probably get by with being late. Larger complexes have management companies who often fire off eviction notices the second day of the month. See what your lease says. Some call for late charges of $1.00 or so for each day the tenant is delinquent; in other buildings a flat 5 or 6 percent interest charge is made for late payment.

If payday falls around the middle of the month, management might agree that your rent can be paid on the fifteenth of the month and not the first. This dispensation should, of course, be added to the lease and initialed and dated by the landlord.

Tenants moving to a new area, or those taking apartments for the first time, ought to call the tenant organization or rent office in their area for information about rent patterns and regulations in the community before they start apartment hunting. Those people can introduce the tenant to the wonderful world of rent control, rent stabilization, rent leveling, and federal guidelines.

Repairs and maintenance: who's responsible?

The law is extremely complicated in the area of a landlord's responsibility for repairs vs. the tenant's. Generally, a landlord must fix anything he promised to in the lease or written or oral agreement. He must also keep public areas, such as hallways, in repair. The tenant is responsible for keeping things shipshape in his own apartment, and for repairing any damage caused by his own negligence or carelessness.

Thus if you break the kitchen stove by throwing matches into the pilot light when switching on the oven, you fix the stove. If it is just plain worn out, it could be up to the landlord to try to patch it up or get you a new one. Also, depending on the terms of your lease, it could be no one's responsibility and you may wind up fixing it yourself. See how well defined the "repairs" area of the lease is?

All landlords must provide heat and hot water, garbage collection and major repairs to roof, walls, and so on. Common grounds must also be kept in good condition. Rent-controlled and rent-stabilized apartment buildings call for a few more "required services," but in the main, since leases are drawn up by building owners, there is very little they are going to fix voluntarily. So if the shower has been broken for weeks, you can complain all you want, but the landlord is probably not violating any part of the lease. No doubt he should make the repairs, but no one is saying he must. True, some malfunctionings may be housing code violations, but reporting them to the authorities could, at worst, find *you* dealing with a retaliatory eviction attempt and *him* with a mere $25 fine. And the repairs still not made. In fact, in some states the landlord does not have to take care of housing code violations.

Sad to say, the overwhelming majority of apartment repairs fall into the gray area where no one is responsible for making them. If you want something fixed, you can ask the landlord to do it. If he says no, you do the job yourself at your own expense. Nonresponsibility works both ways. You do not have to make certain repairs the landlord asks. Also in this amorphous category is the sort of damage to an apartment resulting from natural disasters, such as flood, fire, or hurricanes. Unless the lease says otherwise, neither of you can be held accountable.

Withholding rent when a landlord refuses to make basic needed repairs is becoming a satisfactory alternative to fruitless phone calls and letters. The lease says it's grounds for termination, but if conducted with proper legal advice, it can be done—and with success. The courts are beginning to realize the need for renters to take this drastic action. Early in 1974, the Supreme Court of California (a state known for some of the bloodiest landlord–tenant frays) granted for the first time legal protection to tenants who refuse to pay rent as a protest against a landlord's failure to make adequate repairs.

Some states have legislation permitting tenants to deduct the cost of such repairs from their rent money. But there are certain procedures that must be followed for this tactic to remain within the law.

Finally, there is the "constructive eviction" where in some states a tenant may legally break his lease and move out if a landlord allows the property to become so badly run down that it is virtually uninhabitable; that is, the landlord has failed to provide the basic necessities, such as heat or hot water.

Alterations

Of all the restrictions in the lease, probably of most interest to renters are decorating questions: Can I put nails in the wall? Can I use wallpaper instead of paint? If I come down with a case of ambition, what about paneling and laying tile?

You are supposed to ask the landlord before going ahead with any major changes in the apartment. But if you do go ahead without authority—and how many of us have asked the landlord's permission to hang a picture?—you may be able to get away with it. Take the nails question: In many leases hammering into the wall is technically grounds for termination of the lease. But if it comes to court, it is a rare judge who will side with the landlord. In fact, in one recent ruling on the subject the judge said he regarded "the lease prohibition against the driving of picture or other nails in the walls or woodwork as unreasonable and unenforceable. The apartment . . . was leased for residential living purposes and not as a monastic cell."

However, the unusually large holes and chips left when a massive wall-length shelf system is removed is an example of structural damage that will have to be repaired at your expense.

A way to get around the decoration restrictions that should not offend the landlord is to save what you're replacing. If you put up a new ceiling lighting fixture, for example, set the original one away carefully and then put it back into place when you are leaving.

If the landlord permits wallpapering, or painting in an offbeat color, or even agrees to do the job, you may not have to return the apartment to its original state when you leave. The same for paneling, laying tile or linoleum, or exposing a brick wall. They are, after all, improvements adding to the value of the place.

Make too many of them, however, and the owner may reward you with a rent hike! Best to do major jobs at the start of a long-running lease, not close to renewal time.

Water beds are a new development the lease makers haven't gotten around to yet. Average floor load capacity is from 40 to 65 pounds per square foot. The average water bed weighs 1600 pounds when full. So before contacting the landlord to ask if you *may* install one, check your city's building code to see if you *can*.

"Right of access"

All leases will contain a clause granting the landlord the right to enter your apartment—with or without advance notice—to make repairs, provide extermination, show the apartment when you are leaving, and so on. Protect yourself if you can from what could become a gross invasion of privacy by having it written into the lease that you be given one or two days' notice before those visits are made, unless the repair is an emergency. If the super or landlord is a nosy Parker, there is little a tenant can do. By law these people are entitled to enter your apartment at prescribed times (but they can't *barge* in). However, some visits can at least be at your convenience. Unannounced drop-ins, especially by a cadre of repairmen, can give a tenant that living-in-Macy's-window feeling. One woman came home from work and found a cigarette floating in the toilet. Had the place been burgled? No, nothing was disturbed. A phone call to the super and she was told plumbers had been in that day following up a (non-emergency) repair job on the bathroom overhead.

Evidence of such surprise visits can be, as in the cigarette incident, alarming at first. They are always annoying. Unfortunately, since the landlord has by law a right to enter your apartment to make repairs, and since opening your door with a key is not a punishable "forced entry," there is little a tenant can do against these violations of privacy except to work out a mutually acceptable schedule for non-emergency visits or try to avoid giving him a key and leave one with a neighbor instead, in case of emergency. This may or may not work. Frequently, when you move into a new apartment the landlord already has an extra key. It would be unwise to retaliate against unannounced visits the way one irritated tenant did, however. He is a lock salesman and has found a device that prevents entry during the day when the super or landlord tries to get in. But not granting those two "reasonable access" is grounds for termination of lease. In the event of a burst water pipe or a fire in his apartment, both of which threaten the safety or comfort of other residents of the building, he could well find himself in court.

Breaking a lease

Technically, tenants move, if they do at all, at the expiration of their leases, and they give the landlord the required notice. But changes in one's life do not always coincide with lease renewals. People are transferred abruptly, or drop out of college and return home, or just plain don't like the apartment and want out.

If you live in an apartment-scarce area, the owner might not mind a mid-lease vacancy since he will have no trouble finding another tenant. Similarly, if there is a sublet clause in your lease, you may be able to get out of your commitment that way. A growing number of landlords will accept a compromise solution. For example, if you find a new tenant of whom the landlord approves, he will release you.

Bear in mind that a lease is a legal document and if the landlord is not willing to let you off the hook, you are responsible for all its tenets until it expires. Take off in the night to avoid the obligation, and you may be traced down and slapped with a lawsuit.

Subletting

Not all leases have clauses allowing the tenant to sublet. When they do the wording is still not totally permissive. It usually reads something like this: "The tenant agrees not to sublet this lease without landlord's consent, which consent will not be unreasonably withheld."

Subletting really places the tenant in an awful, Janus-like position. He becomes both landlord and tenant, trying to keep the former happy while making sure the latter toes the line. For if a subtenant wrecks the apartment, the lease holder is responsible. If the sub skips with no notice, back to the lease holder goes the rent responsibility.

Still, there are times when it is necessary to sublet. It may, in fact, be the only way to get out of paying rent on a lease which still has plenty of time to run. Releasing all your rights to the apartment, in which case it becomes an assignment, not a sublease, is another solution. But it is not as common as the plain sublet, where the original tenant is still very much responsible to the landlord. The two terms are used interchangeably, however. But for purposes of this chapter "sublet" will be employed.

Only a handful of states forbid subletting by law. But even if your state has no such statute, the landlord should be approached when a long-term sublet is planned. When the apartment is to be subleased for only a month or two, however, the tendency is often to go ahead and find a subtenant, conveniently forgetting to notify the landlord. A tip to the building's super usually assures *his* cooperation. Co-op owners tend to adopt this ploy since boards of directors usually frown on short-term rentals.

Landlords, surprisingly, do not often interfere with unauthorized sublets. Why? One real estate attorney theorizes it is because they are afraid tenants will report them for violations of the housing code, and it's a rare building these days that does not have some violations.

In some areas it may be against the law to make a profit on a sublet, and in rent-controlled apartments the landlord is usually entitled to a 10 percent rent increase for subletting. So often the profit picture on the transaction is nil for the tenant.

If you are moving in as a subtenant, be sure to look over the original tenant's lease to see that he is not offering you the apartment when he has no right to do so. In fact, if you're staying for a while, ask for a xerox copy of the lease and a copy of the landlord's written permission for the sublease.

Renewal

Whether you will be asked to sign a new lease when the existing one runs out depends on the owner. Some will insist on it and often with a rent increase. In rent-controlled buildings your lease will probably be automatically renewed from one year to the next. Then you become a "statutory tenant," still protected by the terms of the original lease. In other buildings staying on without a lease will make you a "holdover tenant." In such cases the law in some states says the lease remains in effect for another identical term; other states say the lease is in effect from month to month. And in still other states you can remain in the apartment only as long as the landlord allows you.

If you are signing a new lease, and you're in a tight rental area, it might be wise to ask for a three-year lease term as a hedge against inflationary rent increases.

Eviction

Full-fledged evictions—the whole furniture-on-the-street scenario—are rarer than you think. Judges are loath to resort to such drastic solutions to a landlord's complaint, although sometimes landlords don't wait for a court decision and try to force a tenant out by changing the door locks and not giving the tenant a key, or by asking for enormous rent increases.

Legitimate grounds for eviction differ from one state to another, but broadly speaking they fall into two categories: failure to pay rent and everything else. For the former, all the landlord really wants is your back rent, not an empty apartment. Pay up and the eviction proceedings will be halted. (Rent withholding with the sanction of the court is, of course, another matter.) In the other instances, the landlord does want you out, but these too are not that common and the tenant often has some recourse. Rent-controlled apartment dwellers are usually better protected against eviction than other renters, and those holding leases of any type are better off than those without.

Other grounds, besides non-payment of rent, the landlord might have for wanting you out:

• violating the lease and not correcting the violation after being warned;

• causing damage to the apartment or interfering with the comfort or safety of the landlord or the other residents (persistent noisy parties, for example);

• the landlord "in good faith" needs the apartment for his own purposes, usually for use by his family;

• in public housing, arrest (but not necessarily conviction) of any member of a family in residence;

• the landlord wants to demolish the building;

• eminent domain—some local authority wants the building or land for public use (usually tenants in this case are offered a financial settlement or relocation);

• you have not allowed the landlord "reasonable access" to the apartment for repairs, emergencies, and so on;

• the landlord plans extensive renovations that would radically change the appearance and character of the building, switching it, say, from an apartment-hotel to a cooperative;

• you have been charged with/convicted of using the apartment for illegal purposes—such as drugs, prostitution, or arms storage. One "pot bust," although it might land you a jail term, will not necessarily lose you your apartment. Storing hard drugs could. Illegality and immorality can be decided by the landlord under the "morality" or "moral turpitude" clauses in the lease, but judges sometimes do not hold to them. It is a rare tenant these days who can be evicted for having a boyfriend or girlfriend sleep over, or for having regular, high-stakes poker parties. And it is a rare unwed mother who can be evicted from her building;

• the landlord has defaulted in his mortgage payments on the building (judges tend not to be hard on tenants in this event, however).

Eviction is a court procedure and there are prescribed steps a landlord must follow in securing one. He must go to court and bring an action called "unlawful detainer." If you do receive such a notice, don't panic, as frightening as the document appears. You will almost always have thirty days to contest the action in court; (in April 1974, in a landmark District of Columbia decision, the Supreme Court ruled unanimously that tenants in eviction cases have a constitutional right to jury trials). However, do call your local tenant organization or a lawyer for assistance. It is better not to fight an eviction attempt alone. Few tenants are that knowledgeable.

Pay no attention to a landlord's scare tactics: "So and so was evicted and you can be too, if . . ."—a form of psychological intimidation that if carried on for months almost certainly means he has no intention of (or grounds for) dispossessing you. He's just trying to break you. Wait for a court notice before worrying.

Judges, you may be surprised to hear, do not always hold to the letter of the lease where eviction is concerned (except in non-payment of rent cases). They may rule in favor of the tenant for what is outright violation of its terms. The courts are increasingly basing their rulings on the realization that an apartment is for living and cold-print restrictions must be made more flexible. If the landlords won't do it, the courts will. Keeping a pet? The lease says no and the landlord tries to put you out? You may win the case *and* the right to keep Fido. The same for sprucing up the apartment beyond what is permitted in the lease. If the landlord hates the cabinets you put in or the flooring or whatever and wants both you and them out, but the judge feels it all adds to the unit's appearance and, therefore, value, you could win. Naturally each case must be considered separately in all its intricacies and no blanket ruling can be made. Too, there are judges and there are judges and a lot of your success will depend on who is hearing your case.

What can very well get you evicted, however, is what legal minds call "substantial violation" of the lease. If in the sprucing up, you tore down a wall—that might cinch the eviction. A late, noisy party once in a while we are all entitled to. But raucous get-togethers three or four nights a week, bothering everyone within hearing, is stretching it.

A word here about one of the meanest eviction attempts: the retaliatory eviction where the landlord seeks to terminate a tenancy because the resident has complained about the building's state of disrepair to local officials, or has formed a tenant union or is lobbying for rent control. Leases offer some protection against this attempt, but renters without them are often out of luck. Retaliatory evictions are becoming somewhat more difficult for landlords to effect, however, as tenants can prove this is the reason they are in court. In thirteen states they are forbidden by law (California, Connecticut, Delaware, Hawaii, Illinois, Maine, Maryland, Massachusetts, Michigan, Minnesota, New Jersey, Pennsylvania and Rhode Island).

But even in states without that legislation, judges are increasingly ruling in favor of tenants in retaliatory eviction attempts. They base their decision on this one precept: The First Amendment to the United States Constitution guarantees the right to free speech and the right of people to assemble. In a housing context, that means tenants may complain about the landlord all they want, and can organize for protest too. Simple, isn't it?

CHAPTER 4

☐

Condominiums

The magic word in homeowning—and home*building*—circles these days is "condominium," hailed as a new housing concept, but literally as old as the Roman hills.

Considering the advantages of the condominium, one can hardly see how this enthusiasm can pall. Developers like them because they use less land than a single-family development and, although they must be pressed to admit it, there is more profit in selling condominiums. Buyers flocking to new developments, some no more than a sales trailer plunked in front of acres of muddy earth, are equally enraptured. They feel they are getting the best of both the homeowner's and the tenant's worlds. Since a condominium purchaser owns his apartment outright plus a share of common facilities and areas in the project, he is building up equity instead of a pile of rent receipts. There are also tax advantages to ownership, and elaborate redecorating can be done without incurring a landlord's wrath.

On the other hand, no condominium owner will ever be seen shoveling snow or patching a leaky roof. The owners' association to which he belongs takes care of those bothersome chores that are the lot of the single-family homeowner. "It's a lazy man's house," said one satisfied condominium owner.

The condominium takes several forms. It can be a high-rise building or it can be a low-rise (garden) or townhouse (few of which are in town) development. The last type was crowned king of condominium forms, popularity-wise, by the National Association of Home Builders. A new hybrid that is catching on is the "quadrominium," which is made up of four apartment units under one roof, with a single entrance. The appearance is of a large private home.

In price, condominiums start at about $10,000 and go on from there to $200,000 and more. The most popular range is $20–35,000. In Florida's Dade and Broward counties, probably the condominium capital of the world, prices start at about $12,000 for a one-bedroom apartment that does not face the ocean. For oceanfront living, purchasers will pay from $60,000 to $150,000 in a new luxury building. But a condominium with a view of the Intracoastal Waterway can be had for $29,000 to $40,000.

Who is buying condominiums?

First there are the people who can't afford to buy a single-family home, a housing stock that is rapidly drying up. With mortgage rates climbing past 9 percent, hefty down payments of 20–30 percent required, and the high sales price of houses, the would-be homeowner is heading for the condominium development with its lower cost and, in some areas, down payments of only 5 percent (although these are rising too).

Then there are married couples without children and those whose families are complete—"static" households. The 1970 census showed that young couples are waiting longer before having children these days. But many of them still want to own property. The condominium offers ownership *and* the ease of maintenance associated with apartment living.

Single people who want the tax and equity-building advantages of homeowning, but who have no need of a large house, buy condominiums. For younger tenants, the construction of "singles" apartment complexes has provided an additional spur to abandon rental housing.

Couples whose children are grown (euphemistically termed "empty nesters" by builders) often seek out "adult communities," where age limits of unit-owners are fixed—usually at forty-five or so—and children under eighteen years of age are not permitted. Besides offering less space to care for than a private home, condominiums ease the transition into apartment living for older people, many of whom are used to years of homeowning.

Finally, vacationers who are buying second homes in resort areas for fun and, hopefully, profit, also buy condominiums. In fact, the only group that would not find the condominium attractive would be families that are still growing.

Part of the attraction is that a "condo" buyer appears to be getting more for his money than the single-family owner. Many condominium projects are in bucolic settings, complete with man-made lakes, where the middle-income, single-family homeowner could never afford to live. People have more leisure time these days, so many projects offer recreational facilities and a style of living that could compete with a resort hotel in high season.

In the small (101 units) planned-unit development of Walden, in the town of Aurora, Ohio, for instance, there is a private dining club, created from a converted barn, for use by Walden residents exclusively. At the more lavish end of the amenities scale is On Top of the World, a 3,000-member adult community in Pinellas County, Florida, with an impressive number of recreational attractions: two golf courses, a pool, a shuffleboard court, a theater, a private transportation system, daily schedule of activities (cruise-ship style), and on-premises courses ranging from parapsychology and creative writing to a new one introduced in 1973 called "A Condominium Education Program." How can a middle-class, single-family homeowner hope to live like that?

However, the Xanadus are not without a few drawbacks. A condominium is still an apartment and that means togetherness living. Residents must follow rules laid down by the association running the project. Then there are the normal irritations of apartment living—noisy neighbors or lack of privacy. Dr. Carl Norcross, in his excellent report "Townhouses & Condominiums: Residents' Likes and Dislikes," surveyed 1,803 residents in forty-nine projects in Maryland, Virginia, and California and found the most common complaints to be: living too close together, noisy neighbors (and especially noisy children), neighbors' dogs, any subletters or renters of unsold units, inadequate car parking, the owners' association, poor construction, and dishonest salesmen.

There is another point to consider about the condominium. Although its building boom shows no sign of letting up, the unit-owner may one day find when he tries to sell that condominiums are a glut on the market and buyers are gravitating toward newer models with the latest fripperies. Therefore, reselling may be fiercely competitive in areas saturated with this type of housing. Whether an apartment will appreciate in value over the years is also still to be determined.

Of course, the potential condominium buyer should keep these negative points in mind, as well as the positive ones.

Background of the movement

The word "condominium" is Latin for joint ownership or control. And, although it may be the housing of the future, condominiums actually date back to ancient Rome, where they were employed to help solve that city's housing crisis—the same problem that is facing the United States and many other countries today. Desirable land, particularly in or close to cities, is scarce today, as it was in Roman times. To house that city's swelling population the Senate passed a law that would allow Romans to own units in multi-unit dwellings.

Condominiums were also popular in the walled cities of the Middle Ages in Western Europe, until walled cities became obsolete and the population was permitted to scatter over the countryside where land was plentiful. From then on that form of housing declined in usefulness and did not reappear in Europe until the first half of the twentieth century when the populous countries of Italy, Spain, Germany, Belgium, and France enacted statutes permitting it. At the same time, England, although it did not enact the same legislation, began establishing condominium "flats."

Next the concept spread to Latin America and finally, in the late 1940s, it reached the United States. Condominiums were not legal in this country, however, until 1951, when the Territory (now Commonwealth) of Puerto Rico passed a law establishing the legal status of the condominium to ease its own housing shortage. That law was further tightened in 1958 by the passage of "The Horizontal Property Act," which governed the ownership of real property under the condominium method.

The concept then spread to the rest of the United States. In 1961 the United States Congress amended the National Housing Act to extend government insurance of mortgages to condominiums. This insurance was provided by the Federal Housing Administration (FHA), which is now part of the Department of Housing and Urban Development (HUD). The FHA does not lend mortgage money, but it insures loans made by private lenders for the construction, rehabilitation, and purchase of single or multifamily housing for rent or ownership. Although most housing loans in this country are "conventional"—that is, not insured by the government—FHA policies usually serve as guidelines for conventional lenders. In 1962, for instance, the FHA drew up a condominium statute based on the ones enacted by Puerto Rico. It subsequently served as a model for the United States in enacting condominium legislation.

By 1968 all fifty states had enacted laws making it easier to construct or purchase condominiums, and the laws are still being strengthened, especially in the realm of the rights of purchasers

and of resident tenants in condominium conversions. The earlier
rulings vary from one state to another, but they carry certain
common elements:

    • Recognition of joint ownership of all land and other areas
within the boundaries of the structures which are not described as
units;
    • Establishment of a contract between co-owners which
cannot be voided or altered without their joint consent;
    • Separate taxation, or taxation of the units individually and
taxation of the purchaser's share of the common elements of the
development on the basis of its value in relation to that of the
other units.

Buying a condominium

The purchase of a condominium is a little more complex than
buying a private home, but it is not an impenetrable maze. The
following is an explanation of the principal points of ownership
that will interest a prospective buyer.

    MORTGAGE   One of the most important differences between
cooperative and condominium forms of ownership is in financing.
Securing a mortgage on a cooperative can still be ticklish because
a buyer owns stock in the corporation which entitles him to live
in the unit. In the co-op the corporation actually owns the
apartment, and some bankers do not want the difficulty of
repossessing in the event of a mortgage default because it would
be the entire corporation that would be accountable rather than
the unit-owner. On the other hand, the condominium buyer,
since he owns his unit outright, gets a deed which qualifies as
collateral for a home mortgage. Mortgages are usually obtainable
from any bank or lending institution, just as they are for the
private home buyer. Too, many condominium developers extend
mortgages to buyers.

If a condominium unit-owner defaults in his mortgage payments, the bank forecloses, and the apartment is sold to someone else. This system is much neater than the cooperative, where all the owners start worrying when one of their neighbors loses his job, for if he can't meet his mortgage payment, they are *all* responsible.

Mortgage terms vary according to the use of the condominium. A year-round home may qualify for a twenty-five to thirty-year mortgage, with the usual down payment (now 30 percent) that the buyer would put on a single-family home, although some apartment projects are offering initial payments as low as 5 or 10 percent. The interest rates are the same as for the single-family homeowner. Buyers who plan to use their homes as principal residences can also qualify for mortgages insured by the Federal Housing Administration, which may also reduce the down payment.

Vacation-home mortgages are treated somewhat differently. Most banks will allow financing for only ten years on a condominium unit that will not be used through the year by the owner.

Not of mortgage concern, but in the area of ownership, older condominium buyers should watch out for what is called "life estate" buying terms. This means you are buying the use of the property during your lifetime only. Upon death all rights cease, and the townhouse or condominium becomes the property of the company that sold it, without payment. The company then resells it to someone else. *Buyers in retirement communities should read their contracts carefully for mention of this practice.*

CLOSING OR SETTLEMENT COSTS   In addition to the price of a unit and its undivided interest in the common estate, you will be required to pay a mortgage service charge. You must also pay for title search, insurance, and transfer or ownership charges when the unit is resold or refinanced.

UTILITIES   Unit-owners pay their own heat, gas, electric, and air-conditioning charges just as they would in a single-family home. An exception would be high-rise buildings with a common heating or air-conditioning unit.

PROPERTY TAXES   Real estate taxes are also assessed on the individual unit and are paid directly by the apartment owner.

MAINTENANCE CHARGE   You will be required to pay a percentage of common estate costs each month. These include water, sewage, garbage disposal and the upkeep of the grounds (grass cutting, snow removal, exterior painting). Not having to bother with those tasks is one of the attractions of condominium living, especially if you are planning to use your apartment only part of the year and do not want to worry about upkeep in your absence.

Maintenance charges can range from $15 to $1,000 or more a month, depending on the size, location, and elegance of the unit. Generally they approximate what rent would be for a similar apartment.

Although your mortgage payment is sent directly to a bank or other lending institution, the maintenance check, sometimes referred to as "rent," goes to the association running the condominium, all of which means two separate checks each month.

TAX ADVANTAGES   As a condominium owner you are entitled to income tax deductions comparable to those of a private homeowner for expenses incurred in maintaining your property. But if your apartment is in a resort area, and you rent it for part of the year, you may claim additional deductions. More about them later.

First, the unit-owner who lives in his apartment year round may deduct from his overall income the interest he pays on his mortgage. He may also deduct the amount of his real estate taxes, plus any other taxes or assessments made against his property.

A hairline distinction between some high-rise or garden condominiums and townhouse or cluster developments should be noted here with regard to tax breaks, which are different for each type of condominium, even though all may correctly be called "condominiums." For example, the condominium buyer's deed includes "an undivided fractional interest" in the common areas and common facilities. However, the buyer in a project with a homeowners' association (which is usually a townhouse community, a planned-unit development or another form of attached or detached housing) gets a deed that covers his home and in addition—sometimes through a stock purchase—buys membership in the association which owns the common areas. This difference is slight, but the Internal Revenue Service allows the deduction of all interest and taxes for the condominium but will not allow the deduction of the portion of interest and taxes applicable to common areas owned by a homeowners' association, which it views as a club.

Back to tax breaks: Profits from the sale of a condominium unit used as a principal residence are taxed under the capital gains theory. The tax payment upon a profit can therefore be postponed if, within one year, another residence is purchased and occupied.

Condominium sellers over sixty-five years of age may avoid the tax on the profit of the first $20,000 if they have used the unit as their principal residence for at least five of the eight years preceding the day of the sale. They are not, however, entitled to the property tax deduction allowed certain single-family homeowners over sixty-five.

SELLING YOUR APARTMENT   You are, of course, free to sell your unit to anyone you choose and at any time you choose. Many condominiums, however, hold the right of first refusal. This means you must present the name of your buyer to the association and if they choose they can match his offer. The contract clause was set up to protect the condominium from undesirable commercial interests getting a toehold in the community and changing its character. However, it is dwindling in use these days.

Who runs the condominium?

All condominiums and townhouses operating under the condominium method have common facilities (grounds, lobbies and so
forth). These are administered by an owners' association which
everyone is required to join by terms of the purchase agreement.
Becoming a member assures you a vote in the decisions of the
condominium and guarantees the council your proportional share
in the maintenance charges of running the project. At the head of
the association is an elected board of managers consisting of five,
seven or nine members. The project developer initially sets up the
association and the voting rights that come with it. These are
automatically transferred from the developer to the owners as
they purchase. Voting power is usually based on a ratio of the
purchase price to the total price of the project, and sometimes on
the floor area ratios. When a certain percentage of homes has
been sold, a new board of managers is elected by the owners and
eventually they take complete control of the association.

In developments of under fifty or sixty units the owners'
association may directly handle arrangements for services and
repairs and bill payments. But in larger communities a superintendent or a managing agent usually handles day-to-day operations. In a new condominium the developer will often appoint a
manager for a year or two until the building is operating
smoothly. After the managing agent's contract expires he can, of
course, be voted out by the board of managers and replaced by
the residents' choice. In a large complex professional management
is almost a must.

A word of caution: In some new developments, and in a few
conversions from rental status to condominium, developers are
writing in their own thirty-year or more management contracts.
Besides giving the developer a form of control over the
condominium, in more than a few instances this practice has
come to mean absentee managing. Not only does this do nothing
for the building, it also costs unit-owners the 6 percent of all

maintenance charges it is usual to pay a managing agent. Naturally, with a guaranteed income, the developer is not going to be too concerned about staying within a budget—or even about selling the remaining available units. Check your contract to see if mention is made of who will manage the project. If no mention is made, ask the developer before you buy. To be fair, in many other instances having an experienced, knowledgeable builder continue to run the condominium may be a blessing to its residents. It depends on his reputation. New owners should have the option of running the building themselves or hiring outside management.

Once settled in their condominium, owners ought to take an active interest and participate whenever possible in the association running the development. Former tenants may find this difficult since they are used to letting someone else worry about roof repairs and faulty plumbing. But now it's a different ball game. An apartment it may be, but you *own* it. And the grounds around it. The owners' association and its committees are making decisions about property in which you have equity.

Good and bad points

All these regulations seem neat and well-structured in print. But how do they work? After all, the condominium buyer has a somewhat unique relationship with his fellow unit-owners. The man who lives in a single-family house may be friendly with his neighbors or not. The apartment dweller either ignores his fellow tenants or joins with them in the common bond of animosity towards the landlord. But the condominium resident, since his ownership of the very lawn outside his front door is shared with everyone else in the project, must develop, if not friendship, at least a smooth working relationship with other unit-owners.

There are initial bugs that must be worked out in that relationship, a few of which linger on long after the grass is in and the trees have grown tall and shady. Take for example a modern, relatively new project on a tree-lined street in Westchester County, New York. The development is probably typical of small, self-run communities of fewer than fifty units. In a newspaper article one of its residents detailed that condominium's troubles.

She said that at first as each new family moved in, the sociability level rose. Every night there was a get-acquainted party. But as tenancy increased, cliques developed. One side wanted fences between the yards, and the other voted no fences. And when it came time to elect members of the board of managers, the partisan campaigning was reminiscent of emotional high-school elections.

That was four years ago. Today, tempers at the condominium have quieted down. Alas, so has everything else. Where there were willing workers in the first year of operation, now committees are desperate for members. General elections are merely perfunctory. Complaints to weary board members are answered with "You're absolutely right. Why don't you get on the board yourself and help out?" That scares away the dissidents. The author continued:

> Some families moved and others have lost their enthusiasm for the real work involved in running a condominium. The board of managers must do the bookkeeping, arrange for insurance, choose contractors for maintenance, landscaping, painting and so forth. They play the hard game of "Who is responsible?" which goes this way: Do I pay for my new underground garbage can or does the condominium? Our prospectus-makers (the nefarious builders) delighted in obscurity and omission.
>
> Small frictions are still part of condominium life. As an example, we have a center mall with grass and trees. In the spirit of compromise—to prevent the lawn from becoming a sandlot and to avoid the institutionalism of "Keep off the grass"—we made a ruling prohibiting such things as bikes, sleds, bats and balls on the lawn. Those parents who keep at

least one good eye on their kids are irritated, sometimes loudly, by parents who fail to notice their offspring sledding down the lawn on three patches of melting snow. We have no problem if a child breaks a window; the parents have always paid. But what is the price of three broken branches of a shrub or two clumps of grass?

Not a totally glum tale. Obviously the author is basically satisfied with condominium life—witness the fact she is still living in the project five years later—but her words do point up the scattered annoyances that will come up from time to time to plague any condominium owner this side of Camelot.

The good points fortunately far outweigh the bad. Dr. Norcross's study found that over three quarters of the residents his group interviewed are satisfied with condominium living at this stage of their lives.* What specifically did they like? In descending order of popularity respondents cited easy maintenance; dollar value; good neighbors; good design of the units; recreation facilities; the total environment; good location; security and, lastly, privacy.

Several of those same attractions show up in the test group's initial reasons for buying a condominium. More than half made the purchase because they were tired of paying rent. To another sizable proportion, condominiums represented freedom from maintenance. Other reasons for buying, in descending order: the fact that condominiums cost less than single-family homes; better environment; recreation facilities; a greater feeling of security in the condominium complex; privacy and, finally, friends that are near when needed.

Shopper's checklist

When looking for a condominium a little more caution should be exercised than in househunting. For all its claims—and it has its

---

* In the East the single-family home still remains the ideal. Satisfaction with townhouse living is strongest in California, where 56 percent of residents say they will stay five years or more. In the East the figure is 36 percent.

very good points—a condominium still means group ownership, and a buyer is more or less dependent upon, if not at the mercy of, the builder and the council running the project to make his life reasonably serene.

In addition, one must be wary of developers with dubious building practices who put up schlocky apartments, often minus the quality features that were promised, then fold their tents and are off. In Florida, where there are an estimated 200,000 condominium units, presidents of individual condominium associations in the Miami–Fort Lauderdale area have formed the Condominium Executives Council to lobby for stricter regulation of builders and their management practices. Apartment dwellers in other areas of the country are also seeking protective legislation, but at this juncture, where rules can hardly be enacted fast enough to keep up with the pace of building, it is, unfortunately, still a *caveat emptor* scene.

There are obvious points to consider when comparison shopping—sturdy construction of the units, for example. But the buyer who wants the best for his money must probe deeper into the workings of the project that interests him, even if it means a little homework and a few telephone calls. He would only have to listen to horror stories of "stuck" buyers to see that the time spent will be worth it.

It is important, of course, to go over every word in the contract and in the offering plan, which can sometimes run to 200 or more pages and which documents the physical layout of the project, the name of the sponsoring group, the bylaws of the owners' association, the facilities that are to be offered, the schedule of property taxes and the obligation of the builder to the unit-owners. But here are a few special items to watch out for.

1) If the building or complex is new, check out the developer. Does he have a good reputation? Has he built other condominiums in the area that appear to be working well? What is his financial situation? If the community in which you are interested is several states away, you might write the Real Estate

Commission in that state to see if any complaints have been filed against him. For local or out-of-state purchases, check the area's Better Business Bureau or Department of Consumer Affairs to see if either office has a file on the builder. You can even check the U.S. Department of Consumer Affairs in Washington, which has collected quite a number of consumer complaints against certain builders.

2) Watch your deposit money. If a specific number of units have not been sold by a cutoff date, will the money be refunded so you need not be tied to an unsuccessful development? Also, down payments should be placed in an escrow account in your name, and not mingled with the developer's funds.

3) Check with the local buildings department to see if the builder is meeting or exceeding the various building code requirements. Of course, he must meet the minimum standards, but a good builder will exceed the code, and you will get a better-constructed apartment. Well-designed double wall construction, for example, can effectively block out noise between units.

4) Also with a new building, look into the developer's criteria for choosing prospective buyers. Does he make background checks, or is a hefty initial payment sufficient?

5) If the building has been in operation for some time, check its financial condition. Is it solvent? Are there enough funds to see it through an unexpected cash crisis?

6) Does the use of the swimming pool, tennis courts, and other recreational facilities go along with the cost of the condominium unit? Sometimes the builder retains control over those amenities and a unit-owner is charged membership fees to use them. For example, an executive who purchased an apartment along Florida's Gold Coast—the section extending from Miami Beach to Palm Beach—ended up paying $1,200 a year for family membership in the project's golf and swim club, an expense he hadn't counted on.

The Florida Condominium Executives Council is trying to fight these practices, which predominate in the Gold Coast (75 to

80 percent have land lease arrangements) and which they consider unfair. Ernest Samuels, president of the council, declares that "there are cases where the developer holds a ninety-nine-year lease on recreational facilities that are inside the condominium apartment buildings. They aren't even in a separate building. You're paying a lease to use your own ground floor." For the developer the recreational lease is a windfall, with unit-owners sometimes paying $50 a month or more over and above their maintenance charge to use the facilities. Sometimes membership is mandatory. Legislators currently are studying the issue of the recreational lease under intense pressure from angry apartment owners. But it looks as though legally little can be done to eradicate the clause. An individual (or corporation) can, after all, under the constitution lease his property to whomever he wants and for whatever purpose he desires, within the law. What might be possible, however, is that the owners' association be allowed to buy out their interest, say after ten years' time.

7) Read the contract carefully to be sure that you can live with the condominium's bylaws. They all have their idiosyncrasies. Some adult communities, for instance, hold down to a certain number of weeks the length of time children under eighteen years of age may visit a unit-owner each year. Residents who had expected to entertain young grandchildren often during the summer, for instance, may be stymied by this ruling. In another instance, a condominium required all purchasers to agree to use the units only as second homes, and that none of the owners would send their children to local schools. Similarly, there may be a restrictive clause in the contract about the age and relationship of occupants of each unit to the owner, or about pets or short-term rentals. Tenants may be prohibited from shaking out mops from the balcony, or from barbecuing on it. You could move into the project and then find you are unwilling to go along with the association's rules. Check first.

8) Does the condominium corporation own the land on which the buildings stand, or merely the structures?

9) Is parking free or is there an extra charge? Is parking

space sufficient? Since you and your neighbors will be having guests from time to time, there should be at least three parking spaces per unit. In one condominium owners sued the builder who promised them forty-seven spaces but built only forty.

10) How realistic is the developer's estimate of maintenance charges? He may set them low because he is responsible for paying costs until the building is filled, and a low charge is attractive to prospective buyers. But when tenancy is completed, he may find running the project is more expensive than he anticipated and charges are substantially hiked, sometimes doubled within a year after occupancy by residents. This increase can cause anger and panic among sharers to the point where they clamp down on expenditures for necessary repairs or improvements. A Beverly Hills attorney dealing specifically in condominium conversions wrote in a trade magazine for builders that the biggest complaint of condominium buyers in hundreds of Southern California developments is that the developer "low balled," or underestimated, the maintenance charge. The result was that owners slapped expensive lawsuits on the building owners for misrepresentation. Be sure you get a reasonably accurate picture of how maintenance charges are likely to rise in the year or two after you move in. Recognizing buyers' fear of escalating costs, some developers have begun to "guarantee" the rate of maintenance payments for two or even three years.

11) What about insurance? Usually, there is common insurance for the common grounds, with owners taking out property and liability coverage for their individual units.

12) Rentals tend to lower long-term property values. Are they permitted in your development? Sometimes the builder holds on to the last few apartments in a project for rental. Or real estate firms may buy units for rental income. Or the owners themselves may arrange for short-term rentals while they are away. Remember one part of condominium living that participants in Dr. Norcross's study found distasteful was renters.

13) Does your contract say that the owner need not maintain unsold units beyond a certain date? This is a tricky,

often small-print clause. When a builder waives responsibility for unsold—and sometimes unbuilt—apartments, owners in residence will have to absorb the costs of maintaining the empty dwellings, as well as those promised but not yet constructed. Ideally, the offering agreement should turn over unsold units to the condominium association to sell. If the project is not selling well as a condominium, does the developer, who at this point still has control over the complex, plan to rent out the remaining units temporarily? If *you're* renting, will your rent payments be applicable to the unit's purchase price eventually?

14) How well is the building managed? Trash strewn about and scraggly landscaping point to a lazy owners' association. Also, although a managing company may oversee routine operations, all major expenditures must be approved by the board of managers of the association. How are they chosen? How do they think, especially about spending money? Ask to sit in on a board meeting to find out.

15) Talk to several people living in the condominium if you can. Do you think you will get along with them? Are your tastes similar? Too much of a lifestyle or generation gap could cause squabbles over spending money or decorating.

16) Watch out for misrepresentation, especially if the apartment you are buying is still a hole in the ground. In one instance a promised recreational facility was converted into a garage. In several others major brand name appliances were promised, but second-rate ones were installed. Some developers even remove all the recreation equipment—down to the lawn furniture—once they sell out a project. Since condominium sales are seldom regulated, anything can be promised in that glossy brochure.

Perhaps the most important advice to a condominium buyer is *sign nothing without first having an attorney read it and explain any parts you find unclear.* That goes for the developer's prospectus as well as the purchase agreement. You may have to be persistent in trying to see the former paper, however. In only four states—

California, Michigan, Hawaii and New York—does it appear to be a regular practice to give detailed facts prior to the signing of the contract. In all the other states, disclosure laws are minimal. The prospectus may be offered at the time a binder is signed or is sent along with the individual deed at the time of settlement. That's too late.

If state laws are of no help to the condo buyer, perhaps federal ones soon will be. A bill requiring developers to register with the federal government and to disclose full details of their offerings was proposed in the Senate on June 17, 1974. Two weeks later, the Federal Trade Commission announced that it would undertake a nationwide investigation of the development and management of residential condominiums. Looks like help for the buyer is on the way!

One final important point. Buyers are usually allowed 15 days to back out of an agreement to purchase. But this bit of news is almost never mentioned in the purchase agreement or, of course, by the salesperson.

The vacation condo

A cabin by the lake or a cottage at the shore still sounds fine for getting away from it all, but there is a trendier vacation style these days—the condominium. Sprouting up in resort areas in this country and abroad, the condominum method makes perfect sense to travelers interested in far-off places, but weary of overbooked hotels and expensive restaurants.

Pick a vacation spot—and if one or more condominium projects are not already in operation, there will probably be signs announcing one soon to be started. Ski towns and beach areas are popular sites. A condominium in Europe, the Caribbean or Mexico is really *le dernier cri*.

A stay at a resort hotel situated next door to a condominium may set a vacationer thinking during those afternoon lolls around the pool. Both structures are handsome and are beautifully landscaped. Both have swimming pools, tennis courts, restaurants, and perhaps even golf courses. There are shops on the street level of each building. Why not buy the condominium, then, and save on vacation hotel bills? And with three-day weekends now in effect it will be possible to get away for a few short visits during the year too.

There are other advantages to buying rather than renting or staying in hotels. You gain equity, there are tax advantages, and the property will probably appreciate in value. And you may be able to rent it out during your absence.

But before plunking down thousands of dollars, remove the rose-tinted sunglasses, settle down with a pencil and notepaper, and play devil's advocate to the plan.

First, will you become tired vacationing in the same place every year? Once you buy property in a resort area, you'll feel mighty guilty spending any free time elsewhere.

Take into account air fares, too, if your hideaway is several states away. Two or three visits during the course of a year could break your budget. Round-trip excursion fare from New York to Miami for a couple with two children under twelve is over $400, *off season*. Other hidden expenses that are often not considered in the buyer's initial wave of enthusiasm are recreation facilities at the condominium. In many cases you must pay annual membership fees to use the pool, golf courses, shuffleboard courts, and so forth.

Think about location. If you're going out of the country, how do the nationals where you're heading feel about Americans? What about the country's economic and political stability? Tranquil island paradises, for example, can become hotbeds of revolution at the drop of a palm leaf. The assassination of Bermuda's prime minister early in 1973 appears to have been an isolated incident of violence and has not interrupted the tourist flow or the treatment of foreigners there. But later in the year a similar story had a different ending. Terrorists went on a killing rampage on St. Croix, largest of the U.S. Virgin Islands. It appeared to be the sadly familiar story of a tourist boom bringing fortunes to investors while the island's native population suffered poverty and unemployment. Within two months after the incidents began, condominiums selling for $70,000 had dropped to $42,000. Bad for the seller, great for the buyer. But who will buy, at least until the situation cools down?

Tax advantages to owning a vacation condominium are the same as for a year-round property—that is, deductions are allowed for the interest on the mortgage, plus property taxes and any other taxes or assessments. If you rent your apartment part of the year you may claim more. In that event you are entitled to deduct from your overall income the cost of laundry and maid service (which is common in vacation condominiums), repairs, fire and theft insurance, depreciation, and the cost of the brokers' fees you pay to an agent for renting out the property. All these deductions, however, apply only to the part of the year your apartment is rented. Thus if you use it yourself for three months of the year, you receive a deduction of 75 percent, covering expenses incurred during the remaining nine months when the place is leased.

The Internal Revenue Service also permits the deduction of the cost of an annual round trip to your haven to inspect it, pay taxes, and so on, *if you visit while the apartment is occupied.* Otherwise it is considered a vacation trip, no matter how much you plead otherwise, and is not deductible.

It is not wise to count too heavily on rental income, although that is how the condominium owner usually rationalizes his new purchase: "It'll pay for itself because we'll rent it when we're not here." Maybe. In a few projects, particularly in communities with a stable year-round population, owners' contracts often prohibit sublets to preserve the character of the community and to avoid transient traffic. (In condominiums where sublets are acceptable —and they are the majority— there is no need to secure approval of your tenants from the other residents, as you must do in subletting a cooperative apartment.) Other places may have restrictive clauses about the age of unit-owners, and subsequently their renters. Children may be prohibited.

The ability to lease your apartment also depends on where it is located. If the area is glutted with condominiums, you are competing for tenants with many other owners, some of whom may live in projects that offer fancier recreational facilities than yours. Seasons count too. Presumably you will want to spend your vacation time at the apartment. If it is in the north, where summer is the peak season, and you plan to be there from August 1 to Labor Day, will the rent from June and July, say $2,000, be sufficient to meet the annual operating expenses you had counted on a rental income covering? Likewise, if you choose a ski community that becomes a ghost town in the summer, you can pretty much forget about renting after the spring thaw. But if there are attractions in the town or surrounding area to draw a warm-weather crowd, you will be more fortunate rent-wise because the amount of time your apartment can be leased is expanded. In Florida and the Caribbean the occupancy peaks don't seem to matter anymore. The so-called "off season" now draws nearly as many visitors as the winter months.

A new wrinkle in the leasing picture is the "rental pool," or "time sharing" method, whereby condominium owners are obligated to rent their units for a specified time and then share in the profits. That's the modus operandi at the recently converted Camelback Inn in Scottsdale, Arizona. The units there, selling for $40,000 to $275,000, are owned and used by the condo owners only four weeks each year, at whatever time they chose. For the rest of the year the apartments are rented like normal hotel rooms. The buyers share in the rental profits.

New regulations by the Securities & Exchange Commission have brought the vacation condo under federal "full disclosure" registration requirements, as in any public securities. The SEC views the type of condo plan which allows the buyer to live part-time in his apartment while obtaining income from it when he is not there as a speculative interest. This provides some sort of condominium regulation, but it is minimal.

For information about condominiums outside the United States, contact the U.S. Embassy, local Consulate or Government Tourist Office of the country in which you are interested to see how purchases are handled. If possible, it is a good idea to spend some time vacationing in the area before plunging into owner-ship. Several firms in this country can arrange the rental of a condominium, sometimes called an apartment hotel, for a short holiday. Here are the names of a few of them, plus one that handles sales alone:

At Home Abroad
136 E. 57th St.
New York, N.Y. 10022
Telephone (212) 421-9165
(Rentals only)

Condomart International Inc.
655 Madison Ave.
New York, N.Y. 10021
Telephone (212) 751-5400
(Rentals only)

Panorama International Ltd.
810 18th St., N.W.
Washington, D.C. 20006
Telephone (202) 783-3600
(Sales and rentals,
specializing in Spanish
and Portuguese properties)

Previews, Inc.
49 E. 53rd St.
New York, N.Y. 10022
Telephone (212) PL 8-2630
U.S. Offices in Palm Beach, Los
Angeles, Boston, Chicago,

San Francisco, Washington,
D. C., Denver
(Sales only)

Properties International
1631 Filbert St.
San Francisco, Calif. 94123
Telephone (415) 673-3773
(Rentals only)

Do be cautious when dealing with foreign developers who offer all-expense-paid trips to their building sites. A discount on the cost of your flight or accommodations is okay, but totally cost-free inspection tours do not come without a hitch. At the least you will be subjected to a non-stop high-pressure sales pitch that will make the one you heard at that free land-sales-in-New Mexico dinner seem like a genteel lecture by an Oxford don. At worst you may find that somewhere along the line you've committed yourself to buying what they're selling and once on home ground have serious doubts about the wisdom of the purchase.

Again, seeking the advice of an attorney and/or an accountant is important before finalizing any condominium purchase, but in negotiating with foreign companies, it is *vital*.

Conversions

The speaker is the not-so-pleased owner of a new condominium. It is, in fact, the same apartment in which she had lived happily as a renter for many years. As she put it: "I would rather have remained a tenant, but we have so many friends here it seemed easier to stay than to move. But think of all those dollars we hadn't planned to spend!" She is referring to the $25,200 it cost to buy the apartment when it switched from rental status, plus the $500 she was required to pay for a parking space although she and her husband neither drive nor own a car. Maintenance charges, the former tenant added wearily, are higher than her rent had been.

Condominium conversions are becoming increasingly prevalent as building owners realize the profit (25 percent to 100 percent!) they can make in conversion, while at the same time ridding themselves of the headaches and bad press that go along with being landlords.

The owner prepares a conversion plan and submits it, where necessary, to local and state authorities; then the tenants see it. One realty man dealing in conversions advised other building owners how to approach tenants in a trade publication for the real estate industry:

> Don't make mention of the change to condominium in advance; have all materials ready before making any announcement to tenants; explain everything to tenants in person, not by phone; give tenants about one week's notice before putting their units on the market; stress that the terms of their leases will be honored, but by another owner if they don't buy; try not to make an enemy of the tenant—keep going back, always politely and quietly, until you get a decision.

He added that tenant sales should move swiftly, if management has been good, and that the best way to overcome any sales resistance by tenants is to remind them that if the building becomes a condominium, full ownership is in their hands. The writer also noted that another selling point is that building improvements will be at wholesale prices—there is no markup.

The tenant who would like to purchase his apartment when he hears about the conversion plan is fortunate. He is buying property he is already satisfied with, and he is usually offered an attractive sales price considerably lower than the one that will be listed later to outside buyers.

Then there is the tenant who does not want to buy.

Developers estimate that only 20 to 30 percent of the residents of
a rental building stay on after conversion to a cooperative or
condominium, so the unhappy people who want to remain renters
are in the majority. Many of these tenants are elderly and have
neither the money nor the inclination to move. "I'm an old lady,"
said one tenant at a huge rental complex when interviewed about
the rumor of a condominium conversion there. "I lived here
twenty-five years. But how am I gonna buy this place? I got no
money for that."

Tenants holding leases are usually allowed to stay on until their
terms expire; tenants without leases are often told they must
either purchase their apartment within 30 or 60 days or move out.

Does the tenant who is being forced out have any recourse?
Some, but not much. Check first to see if your state has laws
governing condominium conversion. Unfortunately, at this point
few of them do, although several state legislatures have bills
pending. New York has the most comprehensive set of laws—35
percent of the present tenants in a building must agree to the
condominium plan and purchase apartments. If 35 percent do not
agree to buy within a specified period of time, the offering is
withdrawn. It may be submitted again eighteen months later and
usually at that time the price is lower.

New Yorkers fight condominium conversions with bravado. In
at least two Manhattan apartment houses tenants gave building
owners such a hard time over a period of years that today the
buildings are 50 percent rental, 50 percent condominium. Now
everybody's happy. Well, relatively.

Residents of New York State seeking clarification of the state's
condominium (and cooperative) laws can call the special section,
located in Manhattan, of the state Attorney General's office that
handles cooperatives, condominiums and syndications. Their
telephone number is (212) 488-3310. California has a set of
conversion laws too. Tenants can contact the Department of Real
Estate, subdivision section. The telephone number in Sacramento
is (916) 445-6776. Both these offices can also handle harassment

complaints if the landlord is getting abusive about your refusal to buy your apartment.

If your state has no laws governing conversions, there are other ways to get leverage. For example, there is the "bridge mortgage," which most owners have to obtain if they want to convert their buildings. This is simply a mortgage that acts as a bridge between the owner's old mortgage and the new mortgages of the condominium's buyers. The bridge mortgage allows the owner to pay off the old mortgage, release the lien on each apartment unit as it is sold and provide for any repairs needed on the building. But in order for the bridge mortgage money to be approved, bankers almost always require that the building owner have sold at least half of the apartments. So if you all stand together firm in your decision not to buy, the owner may be unable to say that the needed number of units has been sold. No sales, no mortgage. The conversion process stops on a dime.

Tenants-in-residence can also fight the conversion attempt by banding together, by getting the attention of the media, and by casting an unfavorable light on the owner and his plans. (Who is that person trying to dispossess all those poor people?) This may work if the tenants are united, since owners depend on at least 20–25 percent of the original residents buying their apartments—and fast. In fact, one major developer who is converting buildings from the redwood forest to the Gulf Stream waters admitted that if the tenants don't buy within the first month, "we know we have a bomb on our hands."

If organized resistance does not defeat the plan, it will at least get the owner to lower prices to make the apartments more attractive. Resident tenants always get first crack at their units and the difference in price between what is offered them and what is charged outsiders can be $4,000 to $5,000.

Converted apartments should be priced from 20 percent to 30 percent lower than new, modern condominiums. This discount is fair since many old buildings have kitchens with no dishwashers or garbage disposals—all standard in today's apartment kitchens

—and in many cases no air conditioning. This was the biggest complaint of one development's tenants when they heard the conversion rumor: The buildings had no central air conditioning or wiring and odd-shaped windows made room air conditioners impossible. It was one thing to suffer through those summers as a tenant, but they would never *buy* the apartment.

On the other hand, for some unexplained reason, that defect didn't stop the conversion of the North Quadrant of Parkchester in the Bronx, N.Y., the largest rent-controlled apartment complex in the country. The section—3,985 apartments out of a total of 12,072—became a condominium in mid-1973, and its owner, Harry Helmsley and his syndicate, is now attempting, against strong tenant and legal resistance, to convert the entire project. The prices for the apartments in the North Quadrant ranged from $7,400 to $27,200 for residents and $8,510 to $31,280 for non-residents. The thirty-two-year-old complex has no wiring for air conditioning and no central security system.

Buying into a converted building, or buying your own apartment when the building switches, has this advantage: The buyer sees what he is getting, knows the building's history, and can talk to its tenant-buyers. The condition of the structure, however, is important. Prospective purchasers within the building ought to hire an outside engineering firm to make a survey of the heating and plumbing systems, electrical wiring, and so forth, if one is not required to be included in the offering plan. This is vital in older buildings.

A tip to outsiders considering buying in: Try to ascertain how many tenants are buying their apartments. That will give you an idea of what its residents think of the building.

If you feel you've been thrown to the wolves during the conversion process in your building because you had no protection from the state, go out and lobby for legislation that would protect renters in conversion attempts. Organize—either within your building or, as Ernest Samuels did with his Condominium Executives Council in Florida, in a large geographical area. And go to your legislators. Unless they themselves live in an apartment house that is being converted to a condominium, they will have little or no idea what the tenant is up against. As mentioned earlier in this chapter, laws *are* being promulgated to give renters a fairer deal, but the legislative wheels crank slowly. It takes aggressive and determined constituents to give them a push!

CHAPTER 5

☐

Cooperatives

Although lacking the brushfire sweep of condominium construction and conversion across the country, the stock cooperative is
another long-established ownership method that is now enjoying
a renaissance. Today, close to 1 million Americans are living in
cooperative housing programs of some kind. Many of these are
subsidized projects, but a growing number are in the private
sector. The latter category is almost exclusively indigenous to
New York City. Everywhere else, condominiums still seem to be
the leader in apartment ownership styles.

The cooperative is a system of housing designed to eliminate
the profit motive. It means ownership and control of the building
by the people who live in it—not by a landlord. In the
cooperative method, a buyer purchases shares in a corporation
which owns the building and holds the mortgage on it. He does
not own his apartment outright as he does in a condominium, but
becomes a tenant-shareholder with shares of stock in the
corporation and a "proprietary lease" which gives him the right to
his unit. In conventional or privately built co-ops, leases typically
run for the duration of the corporation. In publicly assisted

buildings, they must usually be renewed every two or three years.

There are three types of housing cooperatives:

1) The conversion or rehabilitation project, where existing units are being transformed by the landlord from rental status into a non-profit cooperative;

2) The developer-sponsored project, built with private monies and with the intention of selling all units to be run by the tenant-buyers within two years or so after the first apartments are sold;

3) The nonprofit or limited-profit cooperative, financed or otherwise assisted with federal, state or local aid and frequently made available to specific age or income groups.

The early days

Cooperative housing, as we know it today, did not get underway in this country until as recently as 1920. Around that time a cooperative was started in New York City by a group of Finnish artisans calling themselves the Finnish Home Building Association. Although that may have been called a cooperative, it wasn't until six years later that another project was erected that set the standard for future cooperative housing in the nation. That model project, also in New York City, was sponsored by the Amalgamated Clothing Workers of America. It was called Amalgamated Dwellings and was designed principally for union members. However, other occupational groups were invited to join in order to round out the community.

The movement foundered during the Depression. But then in the years from 1945 to 1961 it became the most popular type of community housing in the country. Its growth in Europe during that time was paralleling our own (and it eventually outdistanced us). The early 1950s were particularly significant years. In 1950

the Federal Housing Act was signed, authorizing the Federal
Housing Administration (FHA) to insure blanket mortgages on
cooperative housing projects. One year later, the United Housing
Foundation was organized. Made up of existing housing co-ops,
trade unions and other nonprofit groups, it is an enormous
nonprofit organization that has developed more than 300 non-
profit cooperative buildings in New York State. In 1952 the
Foundation for Cooperative Housing, the nation's second largest
nonprofit developer, was organized. Based in Washington, D.C.,
the FCH has been responsible for about 50,000 cooperative units
nationwide.

It is important to realize that the cooperative form of housing
has its own distinctive style, one that does not closely resemble
condominiums. The condominium can more easily be compared
to full homeownership than to the cooperative. But since this
book is directed to apartment dwellers, for our purposes we will
occasionally compare cooperatives and condominiums as two
different styles of apartment ownership.

Who runs the co-op?

Residents of the building, of course. But at their head is a board of
directors, composed of from three to nine members, the majority
of whom must be members of the corporation (in a building not
yet sold out, the owner-sponsor will represent the unsold units,
which are usually in the minority—and so is his influence). They
are elected by tenant-shareholders to serve two- or three-year
terms. The board usually meets once a month. They enforce the
corporation's bylaws and alter those rules when necessary. They
consider new applicants to the cooperative, keep an eye on
performance by the management firm, and vote on repairs. They
become, you might say, the building's "landlord." The board can
make some decisions without consulting the corporation member-

ship; other decisions require voting by tenant-shareholders, usually at an annual meeting. Each unit-owner is entitled to one vote at meetings, whether he owns the penthouse or a basement efficiency.

Close attention should be paid to the makeup and workings of the board and to their periodic reports. Remember, they may vote for new projects or purchases you may consider unnecessary or, conversely, they can permit the property to decline by keeping too tight a grip on the reserve fund. In either event you should not idly watch the proceedings. You *own* that building. Participate! And bear in mind a balance must be achieved between changes you all want made and those that can reasonably be made. In one recently converted building some cooperators wanted mail delivered to each door by one of the building's staff and a manned desk set up in the present mail room, but both suggestions were rejected for budget reasons. A sharp, money-saving change saw the doorman eliminated from a side entrance to the building and the tenants given a key to let themselves in.

In some publicly assisted co-ops that are subject to government regulation, more control may rest with the government agency than with the tenant-shareholders, although technically the cooperative management is at the helm. Active participation by residents is not always possible.

Mortgage

Mortgage responsibility for the building rests with the cooperative corporation. There is one big mortgage on the building, or possibly two, which the corporation holds. Owner-occupants make payments on the corporation's debt on a prorated share basis—the larger and more elaborate the apartment unit, of course, the higher the charge. Here is how mortgage and other charges break down for two apartments in the same New York City building.

The unit-owner's monthly check to the corporation covers his

Size	Number of Shares in Corp.	Sales Price	Proportion of Corp. Mortgage	Monthly Maintenance
4 rooms. 1 bath, fireplace	465	$21,101.70	$14,021	$337.13
three rooms, 1 bath	290	13,160.20	8,744	210.25

share of the building's mortgage, plus taxes, insurance and upkeep (repairs, staff salaries, and management fees). This is called the maintenance cost, carrying charge or, sometimes (absentmindedly), "rent."

Those are the expenses for the building itself. If he needs it, the apartment owner must arrange the financing of his own unit with no assistance from the corporation. And that is very difficult to do.

Until the early 1970s, cooperative buyers were required to put up the full cash price for their apartments at the closing, not an easy thing to do if the purchaser did not have stocks, bonds, savings or other assets. There was no financing available at all, for a number of reasons. Banks were not sure—indeed they are still uncertain—whether cooperatives should be considered real or personal property. The co-op lease and stock shares were just not as good a security against default as a deed on a home is. And the mortgage on the building itself, if foreclosed, could wipe out individual apartment loans. In addition, the co-op boards of directors frowned on a prospective owner's need to finance his purchase, since any such loan was to some extent *their* worry too. They were equally concerned about default, especially the loss of their control over reassigning the shares and the lease to the next buyer.

A few commercial banks were allowing personal, uncollateralized loans to help toward purchase, but the interest rate was high

(12 percent), and usually the loans were extended for only five years.

But then, starting in 1971, a few states passed legislation that would permit special co-op financing. The loans—they are still not called mortgages and are still issued from personal loan departments—can now be obtained in New York, Michigan, Maryland, Wisconsin, and Pennsylvania. In New York State, up to 75 percent of the market value of the apartment can be borrowed at 9 percent interest for twenty years. The figure goes up to 80 percent in Pennsylvania, but with no ceiling on the interest rate and a maximum term of thirty years. There is no dollar limit on the amount borrowed in Michigan, Maryland or Wisconsin. Interest rates are 8 percent, 6 percent and 12 percent respectively. In general interest rates on co-op loans will almost always continue to be higher than home mortgage rates.

But, as if the prospective purchaser does not have enough trouble from banks, co-op boards (especially those in long-established buildings) still remain wary of the applicant who requires too much financing. "*I* paid cash," they harrumph.

Maintenance costs

Unfortunately, the idea of buying an apartment as protection from rent increases is one sales promotion bubble that quickly bursts. Residents in cooperatives and condominiums that are entering their second, third, and fourth years of self-regulation are finding carrying charges rising about as swiftly and alarmingly as rent did.

The reasons for the escalating costs are varied: that great catch-all, inflation; original impractical estimate of maintenance costs when the building opened; new real estate assessment, particularly if the structure has recently been converted from rental status; poor initial construction of the building with glaring and expensive defects—a shoddy roof, for example—just coming to light. All these factors have combined to keep the cooperative or condominium resident from the security he had expected to feel in apartment ownership. In a New York City co-op that sold for $11,000 in 1967 with maintenance costs at $211 a month, the charges have risen to $350 a month. In another building the carrying charges went from $250 to $524 in the same period. Since 1967, in fact, the increase in maintenance costs in New York City has averaged over 7 percent a year. According to one co-op board member, in 1973 that figure was more like 10 percent. Rents in the rest of the city, meanwhile, are increasing an average 7½ percent annually.

As an aside to their *Real Estate Review* article addressing itself to banks on the importance of co-op loans, Robert C. Alexander and Margo Alexander provided a chart illustrating the escalation in operating costs in one New York City building. It was co-oped in 1971, and the information was obtained from the building's prospectus.

	1967	1968	1969	1970	Est. 1971	Average Annual Percent Increase
Property Taxes:	32,909	35,220	39,952	N.A.*	55,965	14.6%
Payroll:	46,903	49,635	53,139		70,375	10.8%
Management:	5,416	6,181	6,461		7,560	8.3%
Painting:	4,359	3,975	6,069	N.A.	—	—
Other:	27,825	29,635	34,716		39,950	—
Total Operating Expenses:	117,412	124,646	140,337	N.A.	173,850	10.6%
Debt Service:	30,604	33,000	33,000	N.A.	69,000	22.7%
Total Maintenance:	148,016	157,646	173,338	208,800	242,850	13.5%

* Not applicable.

Added or unexpected expenses, such as a raise to building employees or the higher price of heating oil, will be reflected, of course, in higher monthly maintenance charges to cooperators. In an effort to plug up some of the money drain, some cooperatives are hiring management companies to oversee their spending. Others are firing theirs and trying to save money by running the building themselves. But it is a rare board that succeeds without professional help. A small brownstone co-op, in fact, had so much trouble with its paperwork that it recently was forced to hire a managing agent at $100 a month to take over the bookkeeping.

Of course, there are fixed costs in every building, such as mortgage payments, insurance, taxes, personnel salaries, and fuel. The variables might include management fees, nice-but-not-necessary sprucing up, certain repairs (although a leaky roof or a nonworking elevator cannot usually be set aside until the coffers are healthier).

Management fees for handling all of this are usually based on a percentage of the amount of money the corporation handles annually and range from $8,000 to about $20,000 a year.

What specific services does a co-op management firm provide? They can act as agents for apartment resales. They find and supervise a good superintendent for the building, handle the hiring and salary payments of the rest of the staff, process bills, supervise the payroll, check charges from contractors and repairmen, attend board meetings, take notes and then provide a transcript of the proceedings. One major concern that manages eighty cooperatives did all the scrambling around for fuel for those buildings during the energy crisis of the winter of 1973, one less problem their cooperators had to worry about (and a good example of the purchasing power of large management companies).

Good professional apartment management is difficult to come by, however, in many areas of the country. It is a field that is being drained by the enormous growth and popularity of condominiums in the last ten years.

Maintenance charges, like most other costs, don't go down. The most that can be hoped for is stabilization. Writing for the trade publication *Real Estate Forum*, Louis Smadbeck, president of Wm. A. White & Sons, a large Manhattan brokerage concern, suggests two methods of at least stabilizing maintenance: 1) automate the elevators (a step many buildings have taken), and 2) charge an assessment to the seller of an apartment based on the net profit realized from the sale, a provision that would have to be incorporated in the co-op's bylaws. Those funds could then be added to the building's reserve fund. Mr. Smadbeck suggests a range of from 5 to 15 percent of the net profit after expenses.

The tax picture

As with condominium owners, cooperators are entitled to income tax deductions for taxes and mortgage interest on the building. If they have a co-op or personal bank loan on their unit, that interest is also deductible, of course.

Profits from the sale of a cooperative are taxed as capital gains, so if an owner sells his apartment and then invests in another residence within a year, he can escape paying income tax immediately.

The Internal Revenue Service does not permit co-op owners a deduction for a loss on the sale of their stock in the corporation, even if they have occasionally sublet the apartment.

Residents over sixty-five years of age cannot claim the personal property tax exemption that goes to senior citizens living in single-family homes. When they sell, however, they are entitled to avoid the tax on the first $20,000 if the apartment has been their principal residence for at least five of the eight years preceding the sale.

Normally income tax deductions on mortgage interest and taxes are allowed only when 80 percent or more of the corporation's gross income is derived from tenant-shareholders. But the co-op market has been sluggish. In New York City in particular, some developers and landlords have been unable to fill new buildings or effect successful conversions, so they have resorted to a tenancy that is half rental, half co-op owner. What about the tax deductions in those cases? David Clurman, assistant New York State Attorney General in charge of the bureau that oversees condominium and cooperative offerings in the state, admits it is a delicate area for tax interpretation. But Mr. Clurman adds that most tax attorneys are allowing the deduction as long as unsold apartments are in the name of individuals appointed by the sponsor of the co-op effort and do not carry a corporation name.

Sublet

Unlike a condominium where the owner may sublet to anyone he chooses provided the association allows subleasing, in a cooperative the person subletting and the length of his stay must be approved by the board of directors.

Resale

You may set the price yourself, but the board of directors gets first crack at purchasing your apartment and after that any buyer you come up with must, of course, be approved for membership by those men and women.

In publicly assisted cooperatives where there is a long waiting list for admission, cooperators merely turn in their shares of stock in the corporation and are handed back the amount of their original down payment, any payments allocated to capital improvements, their share in the reduction of the mortgage debt, and a slight extra amount that could be considered "interest." The managers of the building take care of selling the apartment. If the building is in an area where tenant turnover is slow, the cooperator may be permitted to sell the apartment himself. But since the purpose of assisted housing is reasonably-priced apartments from which no one makes money, what the shareholder may charge for his unit is controlled, at least insofar as he may not realize any profit himself. If he sells for a higher figure than he paid, the difference between the two figures is turned over to the corporation.

Good and bad features of co-op ownership

The advantages to buying a cooperative are similar in many respects to those found in a condominium and in home ownership in general. By buying instead of renting, there is, first of all, no worry about arbitrary rent increases (although, as we have seen, maintenance costs appear to be having a mind of their own). There are also tax benefits and the equity buildup gained in ownership. The tenant-owner is free to make structural and major decorative changes in his unit without concern for lease strictures or for tossing money down the disposal on property he does not own. For the timid, a special selling point of the cooperative over the condominium is that one need not sign one's name to a mortgage. And there are no walloping closing costs, perhaps merely a $50 transfer fee at the "lease" signing and, of course, a lawyer's fee for looking over the papers accompanying your purchase. The lack of a solemn closing ceremony, when the new homeowner realizes the enormity of what he has signed on for, can make the purchase of a co-op almost as effortless as moving from one rental apartment to another. Finally, there is enjoyment of a special camaraderie and pride that spring up among joint owners that is missing from those who rent.

Disadvantages? Yes, there are some of those too. A co-op is still apartment living, and that often brings the usual complaints of noisy neighbors, too much togetherness, and so on. And then the cooperative system has its own special peculiarities. Cooperators must, for instance, love their neighbors far more than condominium owners since they are all tied to a joint mortgage on the building. That means if one of you defaults on your maintenance payment, the rest are responsible. However, this possibility is more dramatic in theory than in actuality. Jeffrey Spragens, president of FCH Services, Inc., operating arm of the Foundation for Cooperative Housing and the country's second largest nonprofit developer, says he has never seen a case where shortages from unwanted vacancies resulted in an assessment to resident cooperators. "It's almost unheard of for a co-op not to meet its payments in full," Mr. Spragens says. "Under the federal law regulating them co-ops are required to set up reserves that are more than adequate for almost any contingency."

Then there are the sometimes petty regulations the corporation's bylaws can impose. Reading your lease you may find that the building bans pets or does not allow sublets or will not permit cooperators to have a washing machine. Perhaps there are rules about boarders and permanent guests that could upset your long-established living arrangements.

The co-op board, as stated earlier, approves applications for new residents of the building. For tenant–shareholders, having potential financial deadbeats screened out is necessary and reassuring. But when it comes time to sell, those same tenants may do a lot of foot tapping while waiting for the board *finally* to approve a would-be purchaser who meets requirements for membership.

The practice of screening new applicants in conventional co-ops is a bristly issue, although not as bad as it once was. In the 1960s, during the most recent flush of cooperative fever, the system came in for many charges of elitism and downright discrimination, especially in luxury buildings. Singer Barbra Streisand was refused a New York City co-op she wanted, allegedly because entertainers were "unstable financially and held noisy parties." Patricia Kennedy and her then-husband, actor Peter Lawford, were turned down by a Fifth Avenue cooperative board for the same reason. Jewish apartment hunters were told by agents which buildings they would "feel more comfortable" applying to. And few black or Hispanic co-op owners could be found in any building close to luxury level. Tighter anti-discrimination laws, a sluggish co-op market generally, and what could hopefully be interpreted as a new maturity have all combined to do away with most of these practices. But pockets of discrimination still exist and some shoppers, rather than submit themselves and their bank references to scrutiny and possible embarrassment, choose the condominium method instead. There, no one need know more about the apartment owner than he chooses to reveal, and such discriminatory practices as do exist are easier to prove—and to fight.

Co-op prices tend to fluctuate widely, too, sometimes following the vagaries of the stock market. Although in general for a well-constructed apartment in a good location there should be an overall pattern of appreciation, still co-op prices are not nearly as predictable as those of suburban homes. You may buy high and be forced to sell low. In New York City, co-op prices dropped in 1971 from the hot seller's market of the 1960s and have not yet picked themselves up. For example, James Ling, founder of Ling-Temco-Vought, bought a 12-room apartment there for $520,000 and two years later, in the early 1970s, was forced to sell it for $375,000. Apartments in lesser strata are also often selling proportionately lower.

Caveats for the buyer

When shopping for a co-op it is important to find out who really holds the reins of the building in which you are interested. Sometimes the landlord will retain control until all apartments are sold; sometimes until only a certain percentage are occupied. In a conversion where only 35 percent of the tenants need buy their units, the landlord can hold the remaining 65 percent of the apartments to rent them or otherwise control their use. Offering plans should state that the old owner must turn over to the corporation all unsold units at a specified cutoff date. Otherwise you will have the shadow of a landlord hanging over your enterprise, perhaps permanently. In some cases he may not even live in the building, yet possession of as few as 5 percent of the shares of the corporation may entitle him to appoint a member to the board of directors.

Since few states require full disclosure of co-op offering plans and since the buying procedure is more complex than the purchase of a single-family house, no cooperative should be purchased without legal assistance. Your attorney should read the building's prospectus, the lease, and even the stock shares.

The offering plan should provide information about the state of the mortgage. If it was given for less than twenty years, that's a good warning that the lending institution does not think too much of the building's worth. Does the first mortgage cover most of the principal? If it does not, that's another warning light you and your lawyer should catch. He or she should also be able to find out if there is a lawsuit filed against the sponsor by the tenants—a little information the building's sales office is not likely to pass along in its promotional literature.

Ask the sales agent showing you through the apartment for the building's financial statement for the last five years. That is a good way to trace maintenance costs. It will also give you an indication of the size of the building's reserve fund. If maintenance charges are not broken down, ask for an itemized list to see just where the money is going. How much is spent for painting, what does it cost to clean the pool, etc.?

Finally, it is especially important to remember when checking co-op costs that the sales price of any unit you are looking at may appear deceptively low, particularly if compared to a single-family home, or sometimes even to a condominium. But the asking price does not include the prorated share of the building's mortgage you will be responsible for. Add the two figures together, and the apartment no longer is inexpensive. The four-room, one-bath apartment listed on page 86, for instance, is selling for $21,101.70. A bargain? Look at the next column. The purchaser must also assume $14,021, his share of the corporation's mortgage. So the actual apartment price is a more realistic $35,000.

Does the cooperative provide laundry facilities? Are there enough parking spaces? For other points besides these that should be checked when looking at apartments, read over the "Shopper's checklist" in the preceding chapter on condominiums. Many of those tip-offs can be applied by cooperative buyers as well.

Co-op conversions

It is not difficult to understand why landlords are eager to convert their rental properties into cooperatives. The buildings may not be making a profit, especially if they are rent-controlled and the tenancy shows no signs of moving. The structures may be deteriorating, and capital repairs will soon be needed. Or perhaps the tenants have organized, threatening to balance the long-time feudal relationship. Thus to rid himself of the whole ownership headache, the landlord tries for a conversion.

What is not so easy to accept, however, particularly from the view of the tenant, is the often outrageous price the landlord asks from residents for what is sometimes a downright crumbling structure—and the fact that the conversion can proceed whether the tenant approves the plan or not. If he does not, out he goes.

Regulations governing cooperative conversions are minimal; in most states they do not exist at all. New Jersey and California have some rulings, but only in New York is the turnover process well regulated. There, 35 percent of the tenants must agree to purchase their apartments within six months after the sponsor's prospectus has been approved by the state Attorney General's Office. If the sponsor cannot secure that many purchasers, the plan is voided and cannot be resubmitted for another eighteen months. Other states need those tight restrictions.

Although condominiums are sprouting across the rest of the country, cooperatives are still scarce. But in New York the trend is reversed. New York City, in particular, is the country's co-op city. In fact, the largest cooperative community in the world, a 15,000-family development in the Bronx, carries the name Co-op

City. One theory behind the preference in New York City for cooperative conversions over condominiums has been that it is easier for a landlord to transfer a large mortgage to an association than to individual condominium owners. Blanket financing for condo developments with separate commitments for each unit mean too much paper work for lenders with a limited mortgage interest return that can be charged to the unit-owners. Also, co-op prices appear lower than condos because buyers (and some sales agents) tend to overlook the prorated share of the building's mortgage the purchaser will be responsible for. The particularly militant tenant groups in the city say that the real reason is racist and that cooperatives give the landlord and ultimately the co-op corporation some control over who buys into their buildings, whereas a condominium owner can sell to whomever he wishes.

Besides offering the advantage of building equity to middle- and upper-income tenants and the stabilization of their neighborhoods through ownership, cooperatives have been hailed by housing specialists as an alternative to rotting inner-city dwellings for low-income residents. In New York the conversion of apartment houses in marginal neighborhoods is proceeding nicely and in its small way—like the new "urban homesteading" movement—is helping to forestall abandonment of basically sound buildings. The conversion pattern in those areas offers low-income tenants government-aided financing plans to purchase their apartments.

Cooperatives for higher-income groups have been faring less well. The enthusiasm of the 1960s, where attempts were made to co-op everything in sight, appears to be waning. Not for a lack of conversion *attempts,* however. In 1969 about 10 percent of the buildings offered as co-ops were turned down, according to David Clurman, assistant New York State Attorney General. Today, Mr. Clurman asserts, that figure is closer to 30–40 percent. A spokesman for Tenants Against Co-op Conversion, a New York group militantly fighting conversions, insists the number is "more like 90 percent."

Why the turnoff in a city that has been enormously receptive to the cooperative as a new housing system? Well, for one thing renters nationally—and this goes for those in projects converting to condominiums as well—are beginning to realize the strength of their numbers: United, they can defeat a co-op plan. And more of them want to, especially those in rent-controlled buildings. Landlords' asking prices are sometimes exorbitantly high (although they usually bring them down after the initial tenant horror, and sometimes also throw in a slush fund for any major repairs that might be coming up).

Resale prices, meanwhile, have taken a dive in the last few years, and so the idea of an owner's stability is proving to be another myth. In addition, many of the initial 35 percent of co-op subscribers buy their apartments for speculation and sell shortly after the building is converted; others sublet. The turnover is as high as when the building was rented. But what has probably hurt the co-op process in luxury and semi-luxury buildings the most have been reports from neighboring buildings in the city of escalating maintenance costs. It is quite a financial burden to be saddled with a bank loan of short duration and at a high interest rate, and to carry as well an ever-escalating maintenance charge. Thus a growing number of renters are saying no thank you.

What can a tenant do if the landlord announces he is seeking to co-op the building? In most areas outside New York, very little. The landlord need only wait for the tenant's lease to expire and then refuse to renew it. In New York, there is recourse, although if 35 percent of the tenants do want to purchase their apartments, the dissidents can then only buy or move out. Tenant groups in New York are continually lobbying for legislation that would see the 35 percent figure raised to a more equitable 51 percent, but so far they have had no success. New Yorkers confronted with a co-op plan that no one wants can contact Tenants Against Co-op Conversion, c/o Metropolitan Council on Housing, 24 West 30th Street, New York, N.Y. 10001. Telephone (212) 725-4800. The TACC group visits apartment houses in the city and helps tenants through the conversion fight.

*   *   *

The switch from a rental building to a cooperative is not always accompanied by name-calling, demonstrations, and knock-down fights between landlords and tenants. It just seems so. Some conversions proceed peacefully, although there are almost always tenants who are not pleased with the plan. Those who *want* to buy the building enough to initiate the sale themselves are the most likely to be satisfied. Here is one such story.

Marilyn and Barry Rosenberg loved New York City and their apartment in a handsome old building on the West Side. The street, unlike many in the area, is lovely and historic and is considered prime real estate. But in 1969 the Rosenbergs had a problem that was blurring their Manhattan *joie de vivre*. With two small children the apartment appeared to be shrinking daily. Should they move to a larger one and, as Marilyn Rosenberg wryly put it, "give up eating?" Or to an established co-op which, at that time, would have carried an enormous price tag? Or should they throw in the rent receipts and buy a home in the suburbs?

They did none of the above. The Rosenbergs talked to a few of their fellow tenants and generated interest in buying the building. When the building was co-oped, the Rosenbergs reasoned, they would be able to move to a larger apartment or perhaps put two small units together for more space.

The small group of interested buyers chipped in about $50 apiece for a feasibility study (engineer's report) and for hiring a lawyer who then approached the landlord. Yes, he would like to sell, and there would be more money for him in selling to a corporation than to an individual buyer—a lot more, even if a buyer could be found for a rental building in New York City.

The co-op conversion was not nearly as simple and clear cut as it seems condensed into a few paragraphs of print. It took almost three years. During that time the Rosenbergs and a handful of other tenants held on to the idea while others moved in and out of the building, quarreled, or lost interest.

When the sale was finalized, the cooperators had paid $850,000 for the thirteen-story building. The selling price of six times the annual rent roll was high, but one that is often charged in a prime location. (You can consider 100 to 120 times the monthly rent for an ordinary location reasonable; 130 times or higher for a more desirable building. In ultra-luxury houses in New York City owners are asking closer to 200 times the monthly rent. In general, conversions ought to be priced 20 to 30 percent lower than new cooperatives, allowing for older construction, fixtures, and appliances.)

Besides the purchase price, the West Side group put an additional $150,000 into a contingency fund for immediate repairs and improvements to the building. Fortunately for them, it did not need much. But in many co-ops the reason the landlord had been so anxious to sell is the capital repairs he saw looming on the horizon. In buildings like that the contingency fund should be larger (and the purchase price bargained down, too). At the turreted Dakota, another co-op on the West Side—the setting for the movie, *Rosemary's Baby*—co-opers are now glumly wondering where the money will come from for a $500,000 repair job to the roof and other common facilities.

But back to the Rosenbergs and a happier story. Maintenance at the new co-op now runs from $78 a month for a first-floor studio apartment to $360 a month for the two bedroom penthouse.

Is everyone satisfied with the way things turned out? Naturally not. Some residents thought the purchase price for the building was too high. A few, preferring to rent, moved out. But now that the dust of transition has settled, the folks that are left are pleased with the spruced-up building they now own and are even rather proud of themselves. Especially the Rosenbergs.

One thing the Rosenbergs and their group had in their favor. The building owner sold directly to the tenants. In some cases the landlord sells to another real estate company which in turn "flips" the building to the tenants for a quick profit. The landlord does this not to spite the tenants but because there are tax advantages for him in selling to another single landlord. This way, the original owner also avoids the hassle of working with the co-op group.

Summing up

Condominium or cooperative? Here at a glance are the fundamental differences between the two apartment styles.

	Cooperatives	*Condominiums*
Mortgagor	The cooperative corporation.	Each individual owner who borrowed money to buy his unit.
Mortgagee	Bank or other lending institution.	Bank or other lending institution.
Monthly charge (maintenance)	Proportion of the share of the mortgage plus all operating costs.	Proportionate share of operating costs. Mortgage payments are made separately to lending institution.
Real estate taxes	Assessed on the property owned by the cooperative corporation.	Assessed on each individual unit.
Mortgage term	Cooperative corporation usually has forty years; members are not mortgagors. Members finance their own units with bank loans.	Owner usually has thirty years, same as private homeowner. Condominium is not a mortgagor.
Closing costs	Usual settlement costs when the cooperative first purchases the property. Future members pay only a small ($50 or so) transfer fee.	Mortgage service charge, title search, insurance and transfer of ownership charges.

	Cooperatives	*Condominiums*
Equity	Increase in value of membership certificate resulting from member's monthly contribution toward paying off corporate mortgage.	Increase as owner pays off mortgage and from overall market value appreciation.

CHAPTER 6

□

Security

Man's home is his castle. But the castle these days is taking on the more ominous appearance of a fort. There are bars now on the curtained windows, and expensive electronic alarms at key entry points. The front door has a brace of (hopefully) impenetrable locks running its entire length.

Are such elaborate defenses really necessary? Unfortunately it would seem so. Burglaries around the country have doubled since 1968. There is now one every twenty-five seconds. For apartment dwellers the statistics are even gloomier. The actuaries at Continental Casualty Company predicted early in 1973 that more than 2.5 million renters would suffer insurable loss during that year—and that thieves would be responsible for more than half of that loss. Quite a difference from the lot of the homeowner. Only 12 percent of homeowners' insurance claims are due to theft.

It isn't difficult to see why apartment buildings are so vulnerable to crime. Tenants are often away during the day, leaving the way clear for thieves. There are many units under one roof that can be pilfered and often several entrances to—and fast exits from—the building. Tenants often do not know one another either, so a burglar can pass among them freely.

High-rise projects are more crime inviting than those built on a smaller scale. Architect and planner Oscar Newman in his book *Defensible Space* attributes the crime rate in the multi-story buildings he studied to a lack of "territoriality"—a feeling by tenants that there are no common areas in the building or its grounds that they can claim as a familiar, pleasant and safe extension of their own homes. The stairways, corridors, and elevators are unsafe and offer thieves and muggers any number of escape routes. The residents are strangers to one another. Mailboxes and buzzers are poorly placed in out-of-the-way—and therefore dangerous—corners. Large open spaces that are supposed to serve as "vest pocket parks" in the center of the projects are instead the most feared areas of all. Who will walk through them, day *or* evening, without hurrying to get out of them? Who would ever pause to rest in them?

As an example, Newman cites two housing projects across the street from each other in New York City. One is a high-rise, the other a complex of much older three-story walkups. The tenants in each are identical in income, race, and even density rates per apartment. But the crime rate in the high-rise project is nearly *twice* that in the walkup.

Short of buying their apartments and thus taking an immediate proprietary interest in the common areas, is there any way tenants can decrease their vulnerability to crime? Newman feels the answer lies in better apartment design for new buildings and redesign of existing structures (which is not always expensive). His study team worked on two buildings that fit into the latter category. In one, an old project in the Bronx, the group transformed a feared central open space into a recreation area, modifying the walkways to give tenants a stronger sense of having "their" area and installing sodium lights. The crime rate has dropped to one-sixth of previous levels. In another high-rise, the entrance was remodeled to allow tenants to check at a glance the elevator area.

But apartment people are not twiddling their thumbs until architects get around to updating their buildings. In many instances they are taking the crime-fighting initiative themselves and in the process, probably unconsciously, they are creating the sense of "territoriality" that Newman finds so important. Their approaches are the block association, the building tenant council, and tenant street patrols—all of which programs provide a feeling of neighborhood and ownership even though the residents are not, strictly speaking, fighting for the upkeep and safety of their own property.

What to look for

Before you sign a lease, look for the more obvious security measures in the building. The lobby or vestibule, the hallways, and the garage or parking lot must be well lighted around the clock. If there is a doorman he should be at his post, not running errands for tenants or resting somewhere out of view of the lobby. The inside door should be kept locked, with keys distributed to tenants only. There ought to be a peephole in each apartment door, but if there is not you can install one easily yourself for about $1.50.

Ask the landlord or managing agent showing you through the apartment if there is any central security system—closed circuit television in the lobby, alarms, and so on. Few older buildings have the latest security features unless they have been installed under tenant duress after many burglaries, but many builders are incorporating security devices into new apartment houses to entice safety-conscious tenants. For example, at the Waterview Apartments in Framingham, Massachusetts, when a tenant returns home he must inform an IBM computer in the building. If he fails to do so within a certain time, a security guard is alerted. An added feature of the system is a medical alert button on the control panel in each apartment. It permits the resident to call the lobby for medical assistance.

A different sort of protection is offered tenants at the 200-unit Willowcreek Apartments in Houston, Texas. A city policeman is living there rent free. When he gets home from work, he is obliged to tour the area before retiring. A uniformed police presence, management feels, gives the residents of the development a feeling of security.

What is the landlord responsible for?

When it comes to apartment burglaries, courts have traditionally held that landlords have no responsibility for crimes committed against their tenants. But that appears to be changing. *Apartment Life* magazine reports a landmark decision in a recent Washington, D.C. case. One Sarah Kline was attacked in the hallway of her building and sued the landlord for damages resulting from the attack. A federal circuit court ruled that she had the right, and so Ms. Kline came into some money. "We find that there is a duty of protection owed by the landlord to the tenant in an urban multiple unit apartment," the decision read. The court did admit that a landlord "is no insurer of his tenants' safety," but added "he is certainly no bystander." But before you start dialing your lawyer, read on.

There were circumstances in the Kline case that slanted it in the tenant's favor: there had been twenty-five previous assaults and robberies in the building, and the tenants had complained about security frequently. That comes under the heading of having notified the landlord of trouble. Another point in the woman's favor: When she first moved into the building there were a doorman, a guard, and two garage attendants on duty twenty-four hours a day. At the time of the assault seven years later, the doorman was gone and the garage staff and guard were working only part time. The court considered that a breach of contract between the tenant and landlord.

Some time after that decision, another tenant in the Washington area decided to withhold rent on the grounds that his building had inadequate security precautions. Citing the Kline case, the court ruled against the tenant since the precautions were no better when the tenant signed the lease.

As you see, it is obvious that each case has variables that must be considered, and many tenants will be told they have no case at all. But at least that one breakthrough was made against a centuries-old principle of owner nonresponsibility for persons under his roof.

The tenant's responsibility

There are elementary precautions every renter must take to ensure his own safety. Of prime importance is having secure locks on doors and windows. Burglary data compiled recently by the sheriff's office of Cook County, the Chicago police department, and its suburban bureaus reported that 39.1 percent of burglars gained entry through the front door by forced entry; 25 percent through the rear door by forced entry; 8 percent by means of rear or side windows; 5 percent through an open door. The remaining burglaries were accomplished by miscellaneous or unknown entries.

Other necessary precautions besides door and window locks are using the apartment peephole and buzzer intercom, reporting broken windows or locks to management and reporting suspicious loiterers. When leaving for vacation tenants should stop deliveries of milk and newspapers, the accumulation of which in front of your door will indicate your absence to a would-be robber. Mail will be considered later in this chapter.

But those are just rudimentary precautions. Unfortunately, the escalating criminal population demands that we all go considerably further to protect our hearths—and our lives.

Identifying property

Law enforcement and insurance officials have long suggested that tenants record the serial numbers of typewriters, television sets and other items of value to facilitate reclaiming them if they are stolen. But now there is a better method of identification. Electric pencils can be purchased that etch your name and address on any surface—metal, wood or plastic. A burglar may think twice about making off with an easily identifiable haul. Although the engravings can be filed off, there are methods of restoring them.

The pencils are inexpensive, costing anywhere from $3 to $15. They usually come with free window decals. A suggestion to enterprising youngsters from one manufacturer: Offer the engraving service to your neighbors and local businesses to supplement your allowance.

A more comprehensive identification program is offered in many communities under the label "Operation Identification" or "Operation Safeguard." The plan is usually sponsored by a local civic group working in conjunction with the police department.

"Operation Theft-Guard," the first such program, was started in Monterey Park, California, in 1963. During the first eight years of the program only three of more than 4,000 households that participated reported burglaries. Of the 7,000 households that were not participating, close to 2,000 had been broken into.

Here is how "Operation Theft-Guard" works in one city—Trenton, New Jersey—where the program was inaugurated in 1973. It is sponsored by the city's Zonta Club, and they purchase all the materials. To borrow the engraver, city residents go to the Trenton Police Department where the pencils are loaned free of charge. If they are kept beyond three days a $3 fine is imposed. The homeowner or tenant etches his driver's license number (or social security number if he does not drive) on all valuables. He can think up a special design to use on jewelry and silver. As the items are marked, they are listed on a special form which is then filed with the police department when the engraving tool is returned. The homeowner or tenant keeps a copy of the form. At the time he turns in the pencil he is given two "Trenton Theft-Guard" warning stickers that can be pasted on doors or windows of his home. Additional stickers can be purchased at 10¢ each.

Trenton Police Chief John R. Prihoda suggests that the engraving should be made on such articles as cameras, radios, televisions, clocks, hi-fi equipment, typewriters, adding machines, vacuum cleaners, jewelry and even hub caps—"any items that would have particular appeal to thieves." (Papers and securities that cannot be replaced should be kept in a bank box.)

Nevertheless, it is important not to let warning stickers lead to carelessness in taking ordinary precautions against thieves. An open or unlocked window plastered with threatening decals is ludicrous.

Locks

The first order of business on moving into a new apartment should be changing the door lock. You do not know how many keys to your door are in circulation and who is holding them. Although that might make an interesting premise for a TV situation comedy, in real life it could be deadly. It is not always necessary to change the whole lock; sometimes just the cylinder (the part that takes the key) will do.

But suppose you do want a new lock. You most assuredly will if your apartment has been burgled. Before you buy, however, check your lease. New locks and alarm systems usually have to be approved by management. Look at the door, too. A good lock is little defense if it is installed in a weak door. The door should be of hollow metal or a solid wood and should fit snugly into the frame. A door that is half glass isn't good, but if combined with the proper lock it can still offer some protection.

Next to decide is which lock—and that's a good question. Reams have been written on the subject of door locks, with writers, safety experts, ex-thieves, police and lock manufacturers all discoursing on the more than 13,000 varieties of locks now on the market. Some are good; others are expensive junk that can be opened, as one manufacturer put it, "with a simple slap of the hand."

"Locks are just locks," says a New York locksmith. "When you understand the principle, you can beat any of them." Safety experts agree that no lock is unpickable, but there are designs that are more difficult to break than others. Naturally, the thinking thief will leave the tough ones alone and go on to an apartment with easier access.

There appears to be some progress in regulating the quality of gadgets. The National Bureau of Standards is studying locks with a view toward fixing standards of performance. In California, the Attorney General's Office is conducting similar tests and will release their findings.

But until standards are set, reasonable caution should be exercised when shopping for locks and alarm systems. For the $20 or so you will be spending you are protecting probably thousands of dollars of possessions, not to mention your own priceless life.

The bottom line of all the advice on which lock to buy can be put in a few words: Any door that requires the turn of a key to lock, rather than just slamming, is more secure. Look for a lock with the word "dead" in it—"dead bolt" or "dead latch." Unlike the more ordinary spring latch, which can be opened with a celluloid strip, the dead bolt has a bar extending at least three-quarters of an inch or more into the door frame. Far more thief-proof. For added security, especially if the door has glass, get a lock with a double cylinder, one that is key operated from the inside as well as outside the apartment.

For a good inexpensive cylinder—and Medeco is one of the better buys—you can expect to pay a minimum of $20. The dead bolt, incidentally, is the style of lock required to obtain Federal Crime Insurance.

Chain guards are not effective because the screws can easily be dislodged. Tenants with no peephole frequently use the chain for protection in opening the door to strangers. Don't. It isn't strong enough to deter a strong intruder.

Police (or brace) locks also offer good security. With this style lock a long bolt acts as a brace between the door and floor for inward opening doors. The bolts run across the door for those that open outward. Police locks are especially good for weakly constructed doors that can be opened easily since a burglar will be pitting his strength against the floor and not the door. Professional installation is not needed. Costs run from $15 to about $60.

Some locks require professional installation; others can be put in by any tenant who is not all thumbs. In either event talking to a bonded professional locksmith, one who belongs to one of the national locksmith associations, can clarify what you will find to be an amazingly complex subject. More than 95 percent of locksmiths are honest, but if you do plan to hire one, it can't hurt to check with the Better Business Bureau and your city's police department to see if any complaints have been filed against him.

Alarm systems

Alarm systems can be an equally chancy purchase. They are based on the principle of activating a switch which sends off a loud siren when a door or window is opened. In more elaborate, and more expensive, systems, the alarms are monitored at a call board set up by the manufacturer or the apartment management, or the alarms are hooked up to the local police department. The systems can cost anywhere from $10 for a simple spot wail to thousands of dollars for extremely sophisticated electronic devices.

Two notes of caution if you are considering investing in one: First, before you buy, see if there will be anyone listening. A man in a fourth-floor walkup accidentally set off his alarm at the door to his apartment one Saturday noon as he was moving in some furniture. Not one tenant opened his door to see what was wrong. No one called the police. Moral: you may not be able to count on scared or determinedly uninvolved tenants to come to your aid in a real emergency, even to the point of calling the police from the safety and anonymity of their own apartments.

There is a second point to consider, this one directed at the purchasers of costly alarm equipment plugged into a central station. A recent Department of Justice study showed that 94 percent of alarms answered by police turn out to be false. They are activated by mistake, sometimes from such sensitive influences as lightning or falling leaves. One security specialist says he doesn't have an alarm system in his own home because he knows there are service people who turn off monitors for their customers' systems so they won't be bothered by false alarms. Again, before you buy, make sure there will be someone out there listening to the wail of that expensive equipment.

Windows

Accessible windows—that is, those on the ground-floor level or facing fire escapes—ought to be protected. At the minimum, care should be taken to see that swivel locks are in place when the windows are closed. Also, locks can be made for a double-hung wood frame by drilling a one-eighth-inch hole through both upper and lower sashes where they meet in the middle. If you then slip a sixteen-penny nail into the hole, you will be able to slide the nail back out whenever you want to open a window. But you will feel safer with more reinforcement than that. Stop locks can be purchased which limit window openings to ventilation spaces too small to permit entry, so you need not sacrifice breezes for safety. A broom stick can be cut to fit and placed in the sliding jamb of glass patio doors. There are also specially designed plunger type locks for this type of door.

Rarely will a burglar risk the noise of smashing a window for entry or bother cutting the glass, but if this possibility bothers you, you might consider replacing your glass windows with panes of polycarbonate plastic. It's a tough, practically unbreakable substance. It is expensive, too—approximately $4 per square foot.

Storm windows are good additional protection to a glass pane, but screens are not: they can be cut. Bars and gates are excellent, although they are unattractive and expensive. A metal expandable gate for an average-size single window will cost from $35 to $60. Bars are less expensive at $15 or so a window. But call your buildings or fire department before you buy to see if they have regulations on window protectors. You will probably be prohibited from installing them on windows that are on a fire escape. But there is one style of gate that has been approved for fire escape windows; it opens from the inside with an automatic push-up latch instead of a key. It is called "Protect a Gard" and sells for $60 a window over the counter, slightly higher if you want it installed. It is manufactured by J. Kaufman Ironworks, 1685 Boone Avenue, Bronx, N.Y.

Gates should be considered for ground-floor and rear-view windows and for windows that are exposed to the roof of another building or to a television cable hookup. But save your money and don't bother buying them for fire escape windows that face the street, especially if it is a busy thoroughfare. No burglar is going to do his thing in full view of traffic and passersby when he can be safely climbing into well-hidden rear windows.

If you purchase the standard lock and key gate, be sure to keep the key hanging close to the window in the event you must make a quick exit.

Greenery around first-floor apartment windows can be an excellent camouflage for thieves. Bushes should be kept trimmed and adequate lighting installed around the area.

Fire safety

Fire in a private home is frightening. In a high-rise apartment building the thought is especially nightmarish. But although there are few buildings that offer sensing devices in corridors, or sprinklers or alarms, still the apartment dweller may not be as badly off as he thinks. In terms of construction, most modern high-rises—which, according to fire safety standards, are defined as any building more than eight to ten stories tall—are safer during a fire than a single-family home. For one thing the floors are built of concrete and have a four-hour fire-resistant rating; the walls more than two hours. Too, many apartment fires can be confined to one unit or a single floor. In the average house the floors are wood and there is always a danger of a cave in.

The major difficulty with apartment house fires, however, is that the flames must be fought from within. Aerial equipment cannot be used on tall buildings. In addition, fire department and fire prevention bureau officials say it isn't always the flames that cause the fatalities. The inhalation of toxic fumes and suffocation from smoke can be even more dangerous.

If fire breaks out in your apartment, or if you smell smoke in the building, your first step will instinctively be to call the fire department and, if need be, alert your neighbors. If the fire is in the building, test the door of your apartment before you attempt to leave. If it feels warm to the touch—the knob is a more accurate indicator since metal is a better conductor of heat—don't open it. The corridor will probably be impassable.

If you cannot get out of the apartment, immediately seal the doors with wet sheets and towels and throw open the windows. Seal off the bathroom, too, since smoke can rise through the plumbing shafts. Sit tight and wait for rescue.

If you are able to leave the apartment, take the keys with you in case you have to return.

As tragic deaths in office skyscraper fires have proved, it is foolish to use elevators for exit. Too often they become coffins. Many elevators have heat-activated buttons that will cause the car to stop and open on the floor where the fire is. Or there may be a power failure and the car will become stuck in the shaft. Instead, head for the special fire-resistant stairways or the fire escape. And nothing should be put on fire escapes—they are not make-do terraces.

All doors that open to the outside of the building should open from the inside without a key, and in buildings three or more stories high there must be at least two ways to get out of the building (except in one- or two-family houses or when a special fire resistive construction exists).

Street lighting

From Inglewood, California, to Miami, Florida, from New York to Albuquerque, a growing number of communities are lighting up the night to fight street crime. In the words of one manufacturer, high-intensity sodium lamps are "the hottest thing in street lighting today."

Proponents of the lighting system, which is relatively new, say the intense yellowish lamps bring more people out in the evenings, making for safety in numbers. And the brightly-lighted streets scare off muggers, purse snatchers, and so forth. In Washington, D.C., where more than $2 million has been spent since 1968 to relight 30 percent of the district's streets, there has been a 35 percent reduction in street crime in the relighted areas. In Plainfield, New Jersey, officials place the reduction figure at 65 percent.

Another selling point is that the sodium vapor lights generate double the illumination produced by the more traditional mercury vapor lamps, yet they use the same amount of energy.

The lights do have their detractors. They are not flattering and under them people take on a ghoulish cast. If they are shining outside your bedroom window, they can give the room an 11 AM glow around the clock. Wrote one unfortunate tenant to her local newspaper: "My street, once a pleasant and well-lighted place, now has the nightly aspect of a prison yard. We live close to street level and have scarcely been able to sleep since these glaring, merciless lamps were installed. Street noise has gone up, not down. And why not? Since there is no longer any dusk or nightfall, people roam noisily around until morning." And as for crime in the streets, she added: "The lurid new illumination has brought burglars to my very window sill. Two of my potted plants were stolen the other night."

After considering the pros and cons, if you would like to see your street better illuminated, contact your mayor's office or the Department of Public Works in your city. Perhaps sodium lighting is already planned for your community. If it is not, at least for your block, and officials cannot be persuaded to make the switch (ask in an election year!), residents may be able to change the lights themselves. That's what the folks living in a one-block stretch of West 84th Street in Manhattan did. The street is the usual New York amalgam of brownstones and high- and low-rises. Concerned about street crime, the block workers considered hiring a guard but dismissed the idea as too expensive. They voted instead for better lighting.

Sodium vapor lights are about three times more expensive than mercury to install, but it takes fewer of them to raise the lighting level. The lights for the West 84th Street block cost $1,690—$1,155 for the bulbs and $535 to the city for special pole arms and for installation charges. The money was raised by collecting $5 from each family on the block.

New York City apparently loves the lights. There is a backlog of 200 blocks with pending applications for new lamps, areas that do not come under the city's plan to relight almost 1,200 miles of municipal streets.

Postscript: Late in 1973 Dr. Henry M. Cathey of the U.S. Department of Agriculture reported that a major conclusion of a two-year study he conducted on the subject was that "high intensity sodium lamps are best avoided by most plant life." According to Dr. Cathey, sodium lights make trees more susceptible to air pollution and to frost damage by keeping them growing longer into the fall than they normally would. For example, in Brooklyn's Botanical Gardens in December 1972, the poinsettias failed to bloom. Gardeners were puzzled until they remembered that new sodium lights had been installed on the street where the greenhouses are situated.

So it's back to the drawing board to work out some sort of coexistence for plant life and the strange new lights.

Tips from the pros

There is more to security than spending money for locks, alarms, and lights. The following consciousness-raising advice on daily living in and around an apartment comes from police officials, locksmith organizations, and tenants themselves (both the wise who took care and the foolish who wish they had).

IN YOUR APARTMENT

1) Don't go down to the incinerator room, or to visit across the hall, and leave the apartment door open. Not even for a minute or two.

2) Prepare yourself. Most leases or local ordinances will require the landlord to keep a copy of your key for "access." If you do not like the idea there is, unfortunately, little you can do about it.

3) Don't automatically admit everyone into your building who buzzes. That is how many thieves are effortlessly helped inside.

4) The average burglar picks his victims at random and only about 3 percent will enter an apartment or house where they believe someone to be at home. Therefore, at least the illusion of occupancy is important. If you are going out for a while, leave a television or radio playing. Or even the air conditioner on and humming. Doing this if you are home unexpectedly during the day makes sense too. Burglaries occur most frequently between 11 A.M. and 3 P.M. when, supposedly, most apartments are vacant. You will naturally feel safer during the day in, say, a complex populated by many stay-at-home mothers with young children or

in a retirement community where many residents are around in daytime hours. But discovering that at a certain time you are the only one on the floor in a high-rise, or perhaps even the only one in the building, can be an eerie feeling. Tripping up a burglar's plans was what killed the two young Manhattan women in 1963 in what has since come to be referred to as the Wylie–Hoffert murders. One woman wasn't due at the office until late morning; the other was a teacher on summer vacation. The burglar/murderer obviously did not expect to find anyone at home. This is not to suggest to the probably already paranoid tenant that he should think twice about staying home from work when sick, but rather that precautions should be taken during the day as well as at night. If you can stand it, play a radio near the door. A burglar may suspect it is a ruse, but rather than take a chance he will go on to another apartment. If you go out of the apartment during the day, keep an eye out for anyone you see loitering in the hallways and report him. It should go without saying that if someone is lugging a stereo and a mink coat toward the lobby or service entrance you should call for help. Better to make a mistake and "arrest" the tenant's brother-in-law than allow the theft of someone's property.

5) Dogs are good protection if only for their bark, but do give thought to the size and temperament of the one you adopt. Is it fair to keep a German Shepherd, no matter how fearsome he will appear to thieves, confined to a two-room apartment? It can be equally heartless to keep any dog cooped up in an apartment where there will be no one home for ten or eleven hours a day.

6) If you are in a ground-floor apartment, use timing devices to turn lights on and off when you will be away at night. They can cost as little as ten dollars (or as much as a hundred). Some will even turn radios on and off to keep a steady sound of voices flowing from your apartment. Light timers won't help tenants on upper floors, but they can be useful plugged into a radio or television.

7) Keep a list of emergency numbers near your phone—the nearest police station, the fire department, and the super. Commit

to memory the emergency police phone number in your community.

8) If you have an automatic phone answerer, leaving your name and the message that you are away for a few days is an open invitation to theft. Word the message more ambiguously.

9) Do not talk to strangers on the phone. If someone asks what number he has reached, ask him instead what number he is calling. Never give your name and address over the phone. Another ploy of thieves is the wrong number call to see if anyone is home. And then there's the call where the would-be burglar poses as a burglar alarm salesman, asking if your home is adequately protected. Say no and he'll be right over.

10) Don't let repairmen, salesmen, or solicitors into your apartment without first checking that they are as they represent themselves. Remember, the Boston Strangler was said to have been admitted to his victims' apartments by posing as a plumber. This is one safeguard tenants must be employing in great numbers, however, because many door-to-door solicitation organizations admit they have trouble operating in urban apartment buildings because no one will open a door to them.

11) Buy a record. There is a lively one out now called "Play It Safe." It simulates a husband and wife squabble that should cause an eavesdropping burglar to roll his eyes and steal away (pardon the pun). The record runs for twenty-five minutes and can be set to repeat itself. It is available from Penta Sales Corp., P. O. Box 447, Cooper Station, New York, N.Y. 10003. The cost is $5.98. Then there are records of dogs barking and growling. They are usually sold with warning stickers that can be pasted to windows or doors. The Nova Kennel & Dog Training Academy, 744 Nostrand Avenue, Brooklyn, N.Y. 11216 sells an eight-minute tape cassette (also available on 33⅓) for $2.95. Along with the "Premises fully protected by K-9 Crime Fighters" stickers, the kennel supplies a brochure explaining how the barking can be triggered automatically if someone tries to break into an apartment while the tenant is away.

12) A good protection if you plan to be away for several

weeks is a house- or apartment-sitter. These people will live in your apartment, take in mail, water the plants, care for pets and, most importantly, be a visible presence in and around your home. There is usually no money exchanged (although one suburban woman charges $12 an hour to stay with the plumber, wait for furniture deliveries, and so on). They offer protection; you offer a rent-free home. As might be expected, a few regional agencies are springing up to match both sides. You might also scan the classified advertisements in your local paper and in such magazines as *Atlantic, Harper's, Saturday Review/World, Holiday* and the city magazines—such as *New York, Philadelphia, San Francisco, Atlanta* and so forth—where house-sitters advertise. Or pin a notice to your college bulletin board. References should be supplied, of course.

A spot check of one family of house-sitters and the two homeowners they sat for turned up no dissatisfaction on either side, though well there might have been. The sitters were a young freelance writer, his wife and their two-year-old child. The family arrived on a motorcycle, immediately removed costly bric-a-brac from the reach of the tot, and then settled back to enjoy their stay. They broke only one cup. The homeowners, two couples in their fifties and sixties with suburban houses in the $55,000-plus bracket, checked the couple's references (they are almost "career house-sitters") and then went holidaying without a qualm. Or so they said.

13) Another idea: Why not exchange your apartment for one in an area where you'll be vacationing? Your home is lived in and cared for during your absence and you are saved hotel bills. Two long-established, reputable organizations which handle house swaps are Vacation Exchange Club, 119 Fifth Avenue, New York, N.Y. 10003 and Holiday Home Exchange, P. O. Box 555, Grants, New Mexico 87020. To join either group you pay a nominal $8 or $10 fee to have your name, address, description of property and places you would like to visit included in the clubs' annual directories. Members get in touch with one another via the directories; the organizations' administrative offices do not

make the matches. Almost 90 percent of the membership of these clubs are homeowners, however, so you may have trouble finding someone willing to trade their sprawling eight-room rancher for your Lilliputian studio unless they are childless or your apartment is in a desirable tourist area—the beach in the summer, say, or Montreal during the 1976 Olympics.

IN YOUR BUILDING

1) Do not be smug because you live in a building you assume no enterprising burglar would touch. Today even the poorest ghetto apartment house contains television sets, clocks, and other items that can be fenced.

2) Never leave a note taped to your mailbox or apartment door announcing that you've "just gone around to the store. Back in a minute." You're advertising that your apartment is ripe for plucking.

3) Arrange to have mail taken in while you are away so that it doesn't pile up, another clue to a vacant apartment (although in the tiny mailboxes allotted to tenants, one day's delivery can be an overflow). If the building staff will not hold the mail, or if you do not want to ask them, consider having delivery stopped at the Post Office. Unfortunately, there are a few unscrupulous postal clerks who hand out addresses of vacationers, so you may feel the less *they* know of your plans the better too. If you can arrange it, have a friend take in the mail.

4) If you are a woman, confine the listing on your mailbox or buzzer to J. Jones, not Miss Jane Jones. List it that way in the telephone book, too. Or the mailbox could just read "Jones," and then no one could tell if the occupant lived alone. One woman whose two roommates moved out years ago still has the three names on the mailbox for protection.

5) Hallways must be well lighted. If they are dim, have the landlord buy bright bulbs. If he will not, call your buildings department. Then he will.

6) Never admit anyone into your lobby or vestibule just

because he is coming in behind you. Yes, you may be snubbing a fellow tenant, but he should appreciate your caution. Let strangers ring the buzzer for the apartment they want. In one twenty-unit walkup that was otherwise well fortified, a rash of pre-Christmas burglaries was traced to tenants' politely holding the inside locked door open for the fellow coming in after them. In another building they were holding the door open for a thief disguised as a pizza deliveryman!

7) Stepping into an unmanned elevator with a stranger can be nerve-wracking these days. So don't do it. If you're concerned about appearances, snap your fingers as if you've forgotten something and then step out of the car. If the two of you are waiting for the elevator in the lobby, fiddle around for something in your briefcase or purse, or check your watch as if waiting for someone, and let the stranger enter the car alone. If it's too late and the door closes on both of you, stay near the control panel. If you are accosted, push the emergency button or as many floor buttons as you can.

8) Equally frightening can be a solo trip to the laundry room. Keeping the door to the room locked can help, but that still leaves the walk down to the basement through potentially dangerous corridors and stairs. Best bet is to arrange to do the laundry with a fellow tenant.

9) When shopping for an apartment, remember the top floors are close to entry from the roof and the penthouse with its several entrances is especially dangerous. Skylights are an invitation to burglary and ground floors are easily accessible. What's a tenant to do? Well, middle floors are good. Remember, too, fire escapes that front on the street are safer than those in the rear.

ON YOUR STREET

1) Get your keys out while you are walking toward your building so you can make a fast entry without fiddling around for them out front. One young woman who was mugged in the

vestibule of her walkup no longer stops even to pick up the mail when she is late getting home. She waits until the next morning.

2) Security patrols are becoming more prevalent in crime-ridden areas, many of them tenant sponsored. In large complexes, building owners are hiring special security police. In some areas, people who stay at home during the day are trained by the police department to be "spotters" of trouble in the neighborhood. Where there are active block associations, tenants take turns patrolling their blocks at night armed with clubs. In some apartment buildings they have set up card tables in their lobby where volunteers screen evening visitors. To work, all these programs require a concerted effort by the tenants, and in neighborhoods where special police guards are hired by the tenants, quite a cash output. But police report a definite decrease in crime on patrolled streets.

IF YOU ARE HIT

1) If you return home to find your door unlocked, don't assume you forgot to lock it and confidently step inside. Locking the door after you is a rather automatic reflex, so it is more likely you may have been robbed. Instead of going in—the burglar may still be there—go down to the super and call the police. One tenant glanced into his apartment, spotted the refrigerator door open, and immediately closed the door. (Thieves think many people hide their money in refrigerators!) Do report the crime to the police even if you haven't a hope of seeing your possessions again. Your insurance company will ask if you have done so.

2) If a burglar enters your apartment while you are in bed, pretend to be asleep. He will be glad to avoid a confrontation. Do not attempt to fight if you suspect he may be armed. If he does not appear to be, you can kick, punch, or bite. Do not, however, go for a kitchen knife or a letter opener on the desk. You know who will get hurt!

3) Burglaries should be reported to the super and/or the management of the building, especially if it was their door or lock

system that was at fault. Ask for a replacement *promptly*. The thief could return for a few more items or, if it was an outside door that was forced, to hit other apartments in the building.

But enough of locks, chains and paranoia. It is important to remember that although some 2½ million apartment dwellers will suffer some property loss this year, more than 67 million will not. Look at the doughnut, not the hole! And even if you do become a statistic the burglary need not be totally devastating. There is always property insurance to reimburse you to some degree for your loss. Read on.

CHAPTER 7

□

Insurance

The basic renter's insurance policy covers theft of your possessions and loss or damage in the event of fire, lightning, explosion,
vandalism and a variety of other perils—seventeen in all. It also
provides liability coverage for lawsuits and defense costs. Actually, it is practically identical to a homeowner's policy except that
there is no insurance on the house structure. That is carried by
the landlord.

Cooperative and condominium owners may—indeed they
should—purchase renter's insurance. The cooperative corporation
or condominium association will carry property and liability
coverage for the building(s) and common areas, and sometimes
title insurance, with the costs prorated among residents. But it is
up to unit-owners to protect their own apartments, and that
means renter's insurance (although one company and one state
have introduced special policies for condominium owners. They
will be considered later.).

Is property insurance for tenants necessary?

Automobile, fire, life, and homeowners' insurance policies are written out at a steady clip, and no one would question the value of the protection they offer. But, interestingly, renter's insurance is another story. There are no statistics on how many, or how few, apartment dwellers do not carry property insurance at all, but insurance companies agree that tenants tend to write insurance off far more readily than homeowners.

Some have no choice, being considered statistical lepers by insurance companies. They live alone in a building that has no doorman and work during the day, leaving the apartment unattended. They have been burgled repeatedly, with a different insurance company cancelling its policy after each attack. Or, perhaps worst of all, they live in a hands-off inner-city area that actuaries designate "high crime." They simply cannot get insurance even if they wanted it.

Other renters figure that since they do not own the roof over their heads, why bother with insurance. What's to insure, anyway? A quick glance over their one and a half rooms of personal belongings brings another shrug.

Both groups might reconsider. For the uninsurable there are now policies available although, coverage-wise, they are somewhat limited. More on them to follow. The tenants who consider themselves propertyless might take another look. It is surprising how possessions accumulate. Or perhaps in this acquisitive society it is not so surprising. Even in a furnished apartment there are clothes, jewelry, appliances, sports equipment, stereo, television, books, records, camera, tape recorder, typewriter, silver, paintings. The less expensive goods are usually replaced by those of better quality until lo!, there is plenty to insure. And a devastating material and financial loss could be caused by thieves.

Liability coverage

Then there is the liability side of the tenant insurance package. It is equally important and, too, is somewhat underplayed. Can you afford a lawsuit in the event a guest takes a tumble on your slippery area rug and breaks a few bones? You may be startled to find that even friends will sue in the five-figure range.

Liability coverage also provides for your legal defense if you are proven to blame for the accident. Secondary clauses and benefits of liability coverage differ from one company to another, but in the main they also offer protection for an injury you may cause to someone outside your home, or for your damaging someone else's property.

While discussing who is to blame for accidents, it is good to bring up the question of landlord-tenant responsibility under the apartment house roof. Obviously, the owner of the building carries property insurance on the apartment house structure and liability coverage for injuries on the common areas. If you—or even a guest of yours—slip on a banana peel in the lobby that the doorman should have picked up, the landlord is responsible for your broken leg. In your own apartment, however, it may be another story. If that same guest slips on a banana peel on *your* floor, the lawsuit is all yours. But let's take a different kind of accident. Suppose a steam pipe explodes in your apartment, injuring whoever is there at the time. If the landlord had promised to repair the defect, or is required to do so by law, or did make the repair but badly, he may be required to pay for injuries sustained by some, but not necessarily all, of the persons involved. The law gets very complicated in distinguishing the tenant's invitees from trespassers from licensees, all of whom have different rights, or no rights at all. In the event of an accident like this your insurance agent can advise you what your rights and responsibilities are. Maybe he will suggest you see a lawyer. Leases often have provisions whereby tenants forfeit the right to sue management for injuries. But some courts are waiving this clause. (Incidentally, the *tenant* in the steam pipe accident would probably have no case at all. He waives his rights by continuing to live in the apartment even though he is aware of a dangerous defect.)

Although sold as part of the renter's package, liability coverage can be purchased separately. You can expect to pay about $10 to $12 a year for a $25,000 policy—a good deal, indeed.

Beginning to reconsider the worth of tenant's insurance? Read on.

How much insurance and what will it cost?

The basic tenant's package of property and liability coverage can be obtained from any number of the country's 4,500 insurance companies direct, or from licensed agents or brokers. Rates vary from one company to another and, of course, according to the amount of protection you choose. Do comparison shop, as you would for any major purchase, to see where you can get the best buy.

There are several factors that will affect the cost of your policy and, indeed, whether you will be sold one at all.

• The amount of money insurance companies have spent to settle claims in your area over a certain period of time ("loss experience");

• How much coverage you are requesting and how many dangers you are insured against;

• The condition of your building (if your apartment is over a restaurant, dry cleaner or any other mercantile establishment underwriters consider potentially hazardous, your rates, depending on the vulnerability of the store, may be higher than the tenant who lives in an apartment house). There are other variables, too, such as whether anyone is at home in the apartment during the day, when burglaries most frequently occur.

* * *

All these factors combine to set premium rates. There can even be differences within a state from a "high crime" area to one that is low.

Renters are issued one- or three-year policies, unlike homeowners who can take advantage of the savings on a five-year policy. Still, the premiums on a three-year policy should be less than for a single year.

Annual premiums on the standard minimum $4,000 renter's package of property and $25,000 liability coverage range from $30 to slightly over $50 a year. Payments are made semi-annually. The one charge is lower than it would be if you had bought property and liability policies separately.

James Gillespie of the Continental Casualty Company says nine out of 100 apartment dwellers have some kind of loss every year, and those statistics do not include the many renters who do not carry insurance. The average loss, he claims, is $400.

Not all of that amount can be recovered, of course. Since many losses are under $50, there is usually a "deductible" clause in the policy so that the insurance company does not have to settle petty claims. If your loss is less than $50, you pay it yourself. If it is between $50 and $500, you pay part. When the claim is over $500 the company pays the entire amount according to the terms of your policy.

Apartment dwellers and homeowners who have installed protective alarm systems are entitled to a discount. The highest credit is 10 percent for a system in which an alarm alerts a central patrol service which in turn notifies the local police precinct. If the alarm system notifies the police or fire department directly, the discount is 5 percent. A minimum of 2 percent is allowed for a minimal alarm system of bells or sirens.

Additional coverage

Unusually valuable possessions—expensive camera or movie equipment, paintings, jewelry, furs, antiques, stamp or coin collections—should be insured on a *personal articles floater* or *endorsement* since there are limits to the coverage of those items under the standard tenant's policy. This supplement covers all risks, not just theft. You would even be fully covered if the items were lost (willful negligence, pet damage, and normal wear and tear are among the few exclusions). Each article is listed separately at whatever amount of insurance you choose to carry. There is no deductible. The policy can be purchased separately or as an addition to the renter's package. Rates fluctuate widely according to locale and the articles insured.

Personal property floaters, which insure all your property against any kind of loss (with the same exceptions listed above), are gradually being phased out by many insurance companies. The policies cost almost double the tenant's package and are also difficult to get. "They're just not worth the trouble to us anymore," said one underwriter.

Inventory

Household goods are generally insured for about half their worth (single-family houses for at least 80 percent of replacement value). So it is necessary to take stock of your personal belongings in order to arrive at some idea of their accumulated value. Insurance men have long recommended this procedure, but it is time consuming and they admit that few of their policy holders bother. But it is a good idea to make such a list, for these reasons:

1) Recording personal property, especially listing identifying marks and serial numbers where applicable, will help the police in identifying your articles should they be recovered after a theft.

2) An inventory, although not iron-clad evidence of loss, still can help convince a skeptical insurance adjuster of what you are claiming. If you have no records, no receipts, no trace at all of what you insist went out the window with the cat burglar, your

case will be that much more difficult. The adjuster will have to rely on his own judgment in assessing what you probably did own. If you are a struggling piccolo player and a thief did legitimately make off from your garret with two Andy Warhol originals that were a gift from Aunt Pitty-Pat, you're in for a bad time.

3) Inventory can also show proof of your loss to the Internal Revenue Service. Uninsured loss in excess of $100 is tax deductible. An interesting sidelight to this show-and-tell procedure is described in the book *The April Game: The Secrets of an Internal Revenue Service Agent.* The author, "Diogenes," claims his antennae pick up when a taxpayer comes up with an old sales slip to prove ownership and value of something allegedly stolen: "I suspect he has just happened to find the slip one day while cleaning out his desk. Having found it and having noted that it indicated an amount of money greater than $100, he was suddenly hit by the grand idea of using it in a fake-theft ploy." Of course, if your inventory is well organized and lists *all* your belongings, and if you have reported the theft to the police, you will probably have no trouble convincing skeptical revenue agents.

Proper identification consists of making an item-by-item evaluation of the contents of your apartment. On a sheet of paper, list the individual article in column one, the date of purchase beside it, the cost in column three and finally the serial number, if there is one. Receipts can be attached. If they have long since been discarded, list the approximate date of purchase and cost. New items can be added as they are purchased. No need to worry about depreciation allowances. The insurance company can figure that out from the purchase dates. List everything you own, down to the contents of the linen closet (linens can be grouped as one listing, of course) and the rubber tree over in the corner. If you own many expensive antiques, works of art, and so forth, you may prefer to hire professional appraisers to take stock.

Another method of identification is photographing the apartment from different angles. Prices of the items shown and the dates of purchase can be printed on the back of each snapshot. If you do not have a camera, but do have a tape recorder, walk through the apartment describing the contents for a reel record. The list, photographs, or tape should be kept somewhere other than at home. A safe deposit box is a good idea, or even your office desk. A copy should be left with your insurance agent.

Now for the good, and surprisingly little-known, news for insurance lepers.

Federal Crime Insurance Program

In August 1971 the Federal government initiated a program making low-cost residential and commercial robbery and burglary insurance available to inner-city residents and shopkeepers who had been unable to obtain standard policies from private companies, or whose policies had been cancelled.

The Federal Crime Insurance Program covers "loss by burglary and larceny or robbery, including theft." Its attractions, besides the fact that it is available at all, are that anyone is eligible and that the policy is not cancellable or nonrenewable because of losses.

Policies are now available in Connecticut, Illinois, Maryland, Massachusetts, Missouri, Kansas, New York, New Jersey, Ohio, Pennsylvania, Rhode Island, Tennessee, and the District of Columbia. They are sold by any licensed broker or agent or direct from the company which administers the program. In New Jersey the servicing company is the Aetna Life and Casualty Company; in the other states and the District of Columbia it is the Insurance Company of North America. If you have difficulty getting the policy from your broker or agent because they consider it "small change," go directly to the servicing company.

In some ways Federal coverage is not as comprehensive a coverage as the straight tenant's package—there is no liability or fire (and other hazards) protection, for example—and the cost is high. But it is a worthy program, and for many a beleaguered urban tenant it is the only game in town.

Residential rates will vary according to where you live:

ANNUAL RATES

Amount of Coverage	Territory 1 Low Crime Area	Territory 2 Average Crime Area	Territory 3 High Crime Area
$ 1,000	20.00	30.00	40.00
3,000	30.00	40.00	50.00
5,000	40.00	50.00	60.00
7,000	50.00	60.00	70.00
10,000	60.00	70.00	80.00

The deductible here is $75 for each loss occurrence or 5 percent of the gross amount of the loss, whichever is greater.

Some pluses of the Federal program: It covers "observed theft," which private policies rarely do. This means if a thief gets into your apartment, holds you at gunpoint and then makes off with some of your property, you are covered. *You* must observe the crime, however, not servants or guests in your absence.

Also, coverage up to $500 is provided for loss resulting from forcible entry into a locked automobile trunk. Up to $100 for cash loss; $500 on securities. And, unlike the renter's insurance package, there is no limit on jewelry and fur claims.

There are a few special provisions in the Federal program, however. Except in the case of observed theft, in order to collect a claim a policyholder must prove visible signs of entry in his apartment. That is to say, if you left a bathroom window open and the thief got in and out again with your camera, you are not covered.

You must also have solid locks on all entry doors and some kind of lock on what the insurance companies term "easily accessible" windows. Your locks will not be inspected before you are issued a policy, but an adjuster will look them over after you file a claim. If he considers the security inadequate, out goes your claim. Here is how the Minimum Protective Device Requirement is defined:

Each exterior doorway or doorway leading to garage areas, public hallways, terraces, balconies or other areas affording easy access to the insured premises, shall be protected by a door which, if not a sliding door, shall be equipped with a dead lock using either an interlocking vertical bolt and striker, or a minimum ½-inch throw dead bolt, or a minimum ½-inch throw self-locking dead latch.

All sliding doors, first floor and basement windows, and windows opening onto stairways, fire escape porches, terraces, balconies or other areas affording easy access to the premises shall be equipped with a locking device of any kind.

Jiffy translation of the above by an Aetna agent: "A dead bolt on your door(s) and the ordinary clam-shell locks that are on most windows is okay, and most people already have this type of protection."

FAIR policies

Another program instituted for the protection of the otherwise uninsurable is the Fair Access to Insurance Requirements plan. FAIR is a private, state program offered by a pool of insurance companies. It now operates in twenty-six states and provides coverage for fire, vandalism, malicious mischief and such vagaries of nature as windstorms. But alas, not theft.

As with the Federal Crime Insurance program, anyone can be insured with FAIR, and apartments must also meet minimum security requirements. FAIR rates vary widely, too, but generally tenants can expect to pay about $16 for each $1,000 of coverage. The deductible here is a high $100.

Filing a claim—and losing the policy

Notify the police as soon as you can after a burglary. Your insurance agent will ask if you have. Not that a claim cannot be filed if the theft is not on police records, but it is better for your case if you have been businesslike and thorough enough to report the crime.

Next, think about your loss in dollar terms before calling your agent. You might do better to avoid making too many small claims if you are insured by a private insurance company. They only draw unwelcome attention to your policy when it comes up for renewal. You may find yourself cancelled. If that does happen, though, don't panic. Try another company.

Whether your policy is held by a broker or an agent may also have some bearing on whether you can file without feeling the breath of the cancellation ax. An agent signs contracts with one or several insurance companies and represents only those companies. He can offer you personal service since he is a small operation, but it is important to remember that he, too, is subject to abrupt cancellation. A company to which he is contracted may look over the number of claims filed in his territory during a certain period of time, decide it is too many, and cancel his contract on the spot. Your policy and others in the region are negated as well. A broker, on the other hand, works independently, with no contracts with insurance companies. Since he has no contractual loyalty to any one firm, he can offer whatever insurance he feels is best for you, right up to signing you with Lloyd's of London. And since he has no contract, he cannot be cancelled. But brokers' offices are usually large and impersonal, sometimes too much so for detailed personal attention.

Some agents will try to persuade their clients not to file for *any* claims above the deductible. They say that "the company will cancel you." One respected insurance writer was almost speechless with annoyance in recounting his own experience with a $300 loss. "My agent told me not to report it, that I'd be cancelled," he recalled. "I told him, 'For God's sake, you don't want me to report small stuff and now you don't want me to report $300. What *am* I supposed to report? Nothing, right?'" The writer went on to explain that the reason many agents discourage policyholders from filing any claims at all is that they reflect unfavorably on *their* record with the company and keep them from end-of-the-year commissions awarded to agents who behave themselves (translation: agents who never file claims). Don't be intimidated by this pitch. If your claim is sizable, file. Having an insurance policy where you cannot recover either small, fair-sized or large losses is a little Kafkaesque. Unfortunately, short of changing agents, there is little a tenant can do to circumvent this nasty business—at least right now. Several states have legislation pending, however, that would require insurance companies to renew policies much in the manner of Federal Crime and FAIR programs. That should get those recalcitrant sales people working for their clients again.

Complaints of shabby treatment or discrimination encountered in trying to obtain insurance should be reported to your congressmen, local legislators and the commissioner, director or superintendent of insurance in your state. In addition, write the State Division of Human Rights, the Civil Liberties Union and/or the National Organization for Women about discriminatory practices. The National Organization for Women (47 East 19th Street, New York, N.Y. 10003) is interested in seeing copies of letters sent to those agencies by women complainants. But women should realize that anyone who lives alone, male or female, will have trouble obtaining coverage, since both are usually away from home during the day. "There's no problem about women per se," one agent explained. "If there were two women, one a mother, perhaps, who stayed at home while the daughter worked, I could insure their home."

Condominium owners' policies

In August 1973, the Allstate Insurance Company introduced the first insurance of its kind designed for the condominium owner, and for townhouse owners who own their units on a condominium basis.

All the condominium development's property, except for the individual apartment units, is owned jointly, of course, by the condominium owners. It is normally protected by insurance purchased by the condominium association and the costs are prorated among residents. Allstate's special condominium policy, which reads for the most part like a renter's package, is designed to cover certain hazards that may not be included in the association's policy, or to provide backup protection in the event the association neglectfully allows its policy to lapse. And when an owner increases the value of his apartment by adding interior decorations such as panelling or special fixtures, the policy pays up to 10 percent of his personal property limits for damage to those improvements from an insured hazard.

Condominium owners' insurance also provides loss assessment coverage up to $1,000, which can be increased to $50,000 for approximately $10 a year. This provision protects the owner against many strapping assessments for damage to such common areas as the lobby or social hall. Coverage is also provided against assessments for liability losses for which the association may be liable but for some reason does not pay, such as an injury to a guest in the swimming pool that can be traced to the association's negligence. There is $250 deductible on assessment coverage.

For an additional charge, the policy can be extended to cover the contents of the apartment while it is being rented to another person.

Allstate's condominium owners' policy is now available in thirty-six states, and the company plans to introduce it in several more. No doubt other insurance companies will soon follow suit. A spokesman for Continental Casualty Company said that the firm is studying a similar plan for condominium and co-op owners. "But it's a very, very complicated business," the spokesman said. "Each state has its own laws on what property is common and what property is the responsibility of the individual resident. The condominium owner, for example, owns the paint on his walls, but not the wall."

The Insurance Services Office, a national rating, advisory, and statistical organization serving the property and casualty insurance industry, has also developed a special package policy for condominium owners, titled HO-6. It is already available in Florida and has been submitted to another 26 states for approval.

With talk of thievery, accidents and natural disasters, this chapter and the preceding one on security have probably answered the tenant's question "to insure or not to insure?" Unless one is extremely transient, has few visitors and even fewer possessions, an insurance policy as a backstop to ordinary home precautions makes sense. Apartment living is not, after all, *that* carefree.

CHAPTER 8

□

Roaches, Rats and Other Riffraff

i will admit that some
of the insects do not lead
noble lives but is every
man's hand to be against them

—*archy, the cockroach**

It's a lousy thing to say, but you get insensitive to it. I'm more worried
about the cockroaches.

—High-rise tenant interviewed
following murder and a spate
of other crimes in his building

Late in the evening, when they have exhausted more sophisticated party chatter, apartment dwellers may sometimes be found
exchanging cockroach experiences. Like ghost stories whispered
around a campfire, they are creepy yet delicious.

Take for instance the woman who visited a hotel in Mexico.
She was sitting in a darkened room watching some movies and

* The creation of newspaperman Don Marquis in the 1920s, archy had trouble
manipulating the shift key on Marquis's typewriter. So his reflections read in lower case
letters.

idly fingering a brooch on her chest. Suddenly she realized she wasn't wearing a brooch.

Then there was the New York physician who discovered twenty dead roaches at the bottom of a nearly empty container of grated cheese.

And the workmen at a certain building who sometimes amused themselves at lunchtime by slipping a thread noose about one of the insects and leading him around like a pet. The building was a food processing plant.

The stories go on and on, with each guest trying to one-up the last one. It isn't difficult.

Cockroaches

By every count the cockroach must be the most detested bug on the face of the earth. According to the National Pest Control Association, the roach is also the most important household pest in the United States, a title he has held for many years running. The beast can be found, although rarely, in $100,000 homes, where extermination is relatively simple or, more often, in multi-family dwellings where getting rid of him is difficult, if not impossible. Roaches are, in fact, *the* apartment bug.

He is usually thought to inhabit only slum dwellings, and he is indeed there, doing his thing. But luxury apartment dwellers are plagued, too. One of Jacqueline Onassis' chatty former chefs passed the word along that there were, um, cockroaches in the Onassises' Fifth Avenue kitchen.

Unfortunately, moving to a new luxury building does not solve the problem. Cockroaches feed on the remains of workmen's lunches at construction sites, so when the building is opened they have already been long in residence.

So it looks as if cockroaches will always be with us.

HISTORY OF THE PEST   The cockroach gets its name from the Spanish, cucaracha, and he has been around for more than 300 million years, or as archy puts it: "since man was only a burbling whatisit." The world's oldest extant winged insect, he dates back to carboniferous time—the Coal Age. And, although other insects have evolved into different forms over the millennia, or have disappeared entirely, a cockroach from carboniferous days would be instantly recognized by entomologists—and apartment dwellers—today.

Credit for that marvelous survival record can probably be attributed to the creature's adaptability. Although especially fond of beer and bananas, he will eat anything—food, wallpaper, book bindings, human or animal waste, wood, fingernails or paint. In a pinch, he'll even eat his own cast-off skin. Freeze him and he'll wander off when thawed. Starve him and he'll survive for two months on water alone. Cut off his head—surely the ultimate deprivation—and he can still maneuver for a few days.

Roaches hate and fear the light, but if need be a colony can live quite well, if unhappily, in a brightly lit all-night restaurant. They have been found enjoying life deep in coal mines in India and in South African gold mines. They are virtually everywhere. One woman whose hobby is trying to outwit them as they try taking over her three and a half rooms swears that the good fight will never be won. "When I heard that they survived Hiroshima, I knew we were licked."

The roach's superior defense mechanism also drives his enemies around the bend. Turn on a light in a kitchen at 3 A.M. and watch the action. The insect's speed and elusiveness are two of his more unlovely features. Within .003 seconds after receiving a warning signal he is off and running. Step on him and, like a turtle, he'll retreat under a hard outer shell. Pick up your foot and he's off. Even getting him under your foot counts for points. More likely he will sense the shoe coming down (the message travels directly to his back legs, bypassing the brain), and he scoots off before the shoe hits the floor.

In appearance the pests are usually reddish brown to dark brown in color with hardy, flat bodies, six legs and wings that are seldom used for flight. Two long antennae in the front and two shorter ones in the rear serve as sensory guides. Roach sizes range from five-eighths of an inch to about one and a half inches long.

There are about fifty-five kinds of cockroaches in the United States, but only five varieties are troublesome in buildings. Most of the others live outdoors. The home-loving types are the American and Oriental (or black beetle) cockroaches (they develop in damp basements and sewers and are found mostly on first floors of buildings); the Australian cockroach (develops in warm damp places, in or out of doors, also forages mostly on first floors); the brown-banded cockroach (he's all over the place), and the German cockroach. Once found in certain limited areas of a building, this last type has developed a tendency over the last ten or fifteen years to show up anywhere indoors. Right now he prefers the bathroom and kitchen. The German roach is, in a manner of speaking, the most popular cockroach in the country.

They are all prodigious breeders. The German roach, for instance, carries her egg capsule for about a month, dropping it a day or two before the eggs are ready to hatch. About thirty-seven nymphs hatch from that one capsule. They mature within just six or eight weeks. In her (usually) five-month lifespan, the average female produces seven such litters.

Although considered disgustingly filthy (actually they clean themselves often by licking themselves all over—much like cats), their relation to disease has yet to be proven conclusively. Four years ago two Washington, D.C., allergists found evidence that an allergy to the German roach may be a cause of asthma and other allergic reactions. Roaches have also been known to carry pathogens of typhoid, polio and gastroenteritis, but there is no proof that the insects transmit the pathogens to humans. House flies or certain mosquitoes are more dangerous to health. The pest does have an offensive odor and, like the skunk, he uses it when he is in trouble. (One species stands on his head and emits a fine spray for a distance of up to 7 inches.) The odor and the spray can contaminate food, or even dishes across which the little devils have run. The Washington doctors who conducted the allergy tests found that even cooking food at 212 degrees Fahrenheit for one hour does not destroy the allergy-producing substance left in the German roach's wake.

KEEPING ROACHES OUT OF YOUR HOUSE Apartment units offer roaches a variety of ingenious entries. More commonly they are found in a building's basement or sewer lines and from there they travel through the walls or pipes to exit at any unwelcome location in an apartment. They can also be brought in from the outside in soda cartons, grocery or shopping bags. Visit the basement to do the laundry or to pick up a box of books, and they can travel back upstairs with you in either bundle.

Once cockroaches have established a beachhead in a building they are difficult to get rid of completely. But there are ways of at least keeping them out of sight. And most tenants will settle for that.

The more obvious deterrents are checking incoming parcels to see that the odd bug is not getting a free ride in, and maintaining good housekeeping habits, such as taking out the garbage regularly. But to see your home 99 and 44/100 percent free of them it is necessary to go further. Make it difficult for them to find food. Store edibles that have once been opened (such as bags of flour) in glass or metal containers. Don't leave sticky beverage bottles or cans around; turn them in for money or recycling and get them out of the apartment. Take out bundles of unwanted newspapers and magazines, too. The glue in their bindings is an attractant. Mop up spills quickly and try not to leave dirty dishes or clothing in soak for long periods of time, especially in unlighted rooms. It is the combination of warmth, moisture, and darkness that brings them out.

Scrubbing wood floors and baseboards unfortunately contributes to the problem rather than to the solution. The water that seeps in between the floor boards will either bring roaches out of hiding right there or scatter them so that they surface in other, even more undesirable places. Do check floors, baseboards and walls for cracks or holes, though. A caulking compound can seal them up. Pay special attention to gaps around water and steam pipes. One couple packed steel wool in larger holes and that worked nicely. Also check to see that window screens and storm windows are tight fitting.

PROPRIETARY PRODUCTS   After putting their house in order, most tenants turn next to the supermarket to supplement their efforts. And thanks to roaches being such a nice, steady business, there are products galore to choose from. Some are wistful, a little like the traveling medicine man's wonder potion: a true believer really sees a cure—or at least a change for the better. For instance, one man swears that Mennen Spray Deodorant is killing his roaches. Who can argue? More orthodox products include Clorox, pools of which are supposed to be set in the sink; sulphur candles and assorted powders and traps. One of the more popular fighters is J-O paste, a substance that is spread on a tray or a piece of tin foil (or sometimes a potato) and left near a roach hideout. Its advocates say it works somewhat better than other similar remedies but is highly toxic; do not use around small children.

Then there are aerosol sprays. Professional exterminators suggest tenants with a roach problem pass over sprays that contain pyrethrins, which kill but have no residual effect, and those with DDT, chlordane and lindane, all of which are useless anymore. You may make one lone roach roll over and die, but the fumes will stir things up at the homestead, and there will probably be ten more in that same spot the next day—or worse yet, in ten different spots. Cockroaches will run from an unpleasant odor that isn't strong enough to kill them and head straight for an area they've never visited before. Said one exterminator who gets more than fifty calls a month where the cockroach problem is in the tenants' bedroom: "I first ask the folks if they used an aerosol bomb. I can't remember the last time anybody said no."

If you are determined to spray, pest control savants suggest you look for products that contain diazanon, ronnel or Baygon—all killers that are still reasonably effective. Aerosols with any of those ingredients are extremely hard to find on store shelves, although Boyle-Midway, Inc. is now marketing Black Flag Ant & Roach Killer with Baygon. Here is a better idea: Many exterminators sell sprays to the general public that were made up for pest control operators and do contain a high concentration of the better chemicals. They're also expensive—about $5 a can— but they will do the job better than the milder supermarket or hardware store brands.

And doing the job does not mean wandering from room to room spraying as if with Scent of the Lonesome Pine. Effective control calls for nitty-gritty application. Spray behind the sink, stove and refrigerator, in wall cracks (better yet, seal up the cracks), around the garbage pail, window frames, pipes or conduits and the undersides of tables and chairs. The nasty things love the warmth of running motors, too, so don't forget fans, air conditioning units and behind electric wall clocks. For even better coverage kick panels on refrigerators and ranges should be removed. Drill half-inch holes at the top of panels beneath cabinets and apply the product liberally to those areas, too. Do not spray entire rooms—just areas where roaches are likely to hide. Surfaces used for the preparation of food, or storage spaces that contain food, should not be treated either. Be sure to apply enough of the concentrate to each area. If the mist is too fine, it will float away. Apply to moisten the surface, but not so much that the liquid is dripping. To preserve your lungs, try using a paint brush dipped in the liquid rather than spraying.

One week later, do it all again. Repeating the process regularly is necessary since eggs laid by roaches that have been killed will hatch.

EXTERMINATION SERVICES   If all that sounds too ambitious, consider an extermination service. They will do the job far better than any amateur, and they are a bargain as well.

They are also effective, at least to the degree that roaches can be controlled at all. But extermination certainly makes sense in a multi-unit building where residents are pretty much at the mercy of their neighbors' housekeeping habits and where, if untended, the problem could become uncontrollable.

Rates depend on several factors: the overall condition of the apartment house; the degree of infestation and whether the building is near a food store or above a restaurant. A telephone call to an exterminator usually brings a free estimate. Generally, a 20-unit, reasonably clean building will cost from $50 to $100 for what is called the initial "clean out" of all apartments. Maintenance, which consists of followup visits by the extermination team every month or two, will run about $8 to $10 for the entire building. The followup calls are not made as a matter of rote on all apartments. Only tenants who want them sign up when the dates are posted.

Who pays for all this? In some instances it will be the landlord, who must keep his building vermin-free to satisfy the local Board of Health. If he cannot be persuaded to include extermination as a building service—and by all means he should be approached first—the tenants can band together and split the charge. Individual shares of the bill for that 20 unit house, for example, would run from $2.50 to $5 for the clean out, with followup calls costing as little as 40¢ apiece—a rather inexpensive package.

No matter who is paying, it is extremely important that everyone cooperates in seeing that apartments are accessible for the clean out, since the purpose of that treatment is to get the problem down to a level where it can be routinely handled by maintenance calls. If tenants are paying for the service, a system can be worked out to allow the workmen entrance to all apartments—perhaps keys left with someone who expects to be at home that day.

It is not a waste of money to be the only tenant in an infested building who is calling in an exterminator. Roaches will naturally head for apartments where they are welcome more often than to an area that has become a veritable fort against them. Initial debugging of a two-bedroom apartment will cost about $25, with bimonthly checkups running to $5 or $10.

Exterminators' trucks are usually unmarked, to protect customers' sensibilities. As one pest control man explained: "Sure, we lose some business that way, but nobody wants to tell the world he's lousy with roaches." One wit, though, has managed to make his point by painting a huge bug face on the front of the Volkswagen he drives for house calls.

The men should leave no traces behind them. No clouds of horrible-smelling gunk and nothing disturbed that is not put back into place. However, children and pets should not be allowed access to treated areas until the surface is dry.

Boric acid powder   In the last several years extensive research into cockroach control has turned up what may prove to be the Great Hope of roach-ridden tenants. The discovery is plain boric acid that has been kept in medicine chests for eye wash. Roaches so far do not seem immune to it and, since current experiments date back to 1965, there is reason to believe they will never develop a defense against it.

Dr. Walter Ebeling, professor of entomology at the University of California at Los Angeles, is a prime mover behind the development of the powder as a roach killer. His results have been reported in scientific journals, and have found their way into United States government pamphlets on cockroach control put out by the Department of Agriculture. Until 1972, however, results of treatments with the dust were confined pretty much to the scientific community and a few field areas. Since then the mass media has picked up the good news, and many an apartment is now being blanketed with the stuff.

Boric acid isn't new. The compound and a like substance, borax, were originally used around the turn of the century. But it was slow acting and when roaches were still around six days after application, enthusiasm for it would wane. Boric acid acts as a stomach poison. After walking through the powder, cockroaches ingest it by licking their feet to clean themselves. After DDT and other kill-on-contact insecticides came along, boric acid was forgotten.

But the wonder killers weren't so wonderful after all. A brief flurry of repellency and soon roaches would build up an immunity. This happened over and over again, no matter what the scientists came up with. Dr. Ebeling's experiments showed how the roaches' resistance worked.

The scientist noticed that the traditional way of testing the effectiveness of an insecticide was to put the cockroaches into a container that had been spread with the chemical to be tested and then see how many died and how quickly. To Ebeling that seemed an illogical test. As he explained to *Science Digest*:

> The insect is *trapped* in the insecticide; of course he'll die. But suppose the material *repels* him? In buildings, he doesn't *have* to come near it. The poison may be excellent, but if the roach avoids it, it's worthless. Instead of killing him, it may simply send him to another part of the house.

So Ebeling tried an experiment that would better test repellency. Several wooden boxes—he called them "choice boxes"—were divided into two sections: one was covered with a clear glass, the other closed over and dark. There was a hole between. In the dark side he put the latest insecticide to be tested, and in the clear half he put twenty cockroaches. Now the roaches had a choice: They could dash into the dark, which they loved, or remain in the light, which they feared, but which was safe. A few dashed into the dark side, were repelled by the chemical and scurried back into the light. But many of those who recovered from their bout with the insecticide preferred to live on in the hated light rather than return to the poisoned area. They learned.

Next came the same trial with boric acid in the dark box. Now, Ebeling found, the insects didn't mind running through it. It was odorless and they weren't aware it was lethal. This was probably the most important discovery in Ebeling's research.

More tests in the laboratory and in selected Los Angeles homes and Dr. Ebeling was ready for a field test. He chose seven infested apartment houses run by the San Francisco Housing

Authority. With the assistance of the city's pest control team, he first trapped as many roaches as he could to get an estimate of their overall number, then treated each of the buildings with a different insecticide. The buildings were watched for three months.

A month after dusting, the building that had had the boric acid treatment showed less than one percent as many roaches as before the experiment. The other buildings contained from 7.5 to 11 percent the original number of roaches. In one, the roach population eventually doubled.

Today, the San Francisco Housing Authority still depends on boric acid to keep its buildings roach free. The news of their success has since spread to other California communities. In Pasadena, free extermination is now offered to residents by the non-profit Pasadena Information Center under the direction of Michael Zinzun. The slogan of the group: "Off the Roach." Powder and spray guns used for application have been donated by local merchants. Mr. Zinzun and his crew also hand out flyers on followup preventive measures to homeowners and tenants they visit.

Treating a home with boric acid works in much the same way as spraying with an aerosol can. It is important to reach all the pests' hideouts. Use a plastic squeeze bottle or a bulb duster to treat the problem areas. The stuff can be purchased at drugstores in pure form or at hardware stores or chemical supply houses where it is usually mixed with an additive that prevents it from caking. Since the powder does not decompose rapidly it is effective as long as it is left in place. For esthetic reasons, however, you may want to sweep it up occasionally and put down a fresh supply. One or two pounds will do for effective application, depending on the size of the apartment.

Results will not be evident overnight. But in two weeks' time you should see a snow-covered corpse or two. Or if you do spot a living roach he will be moving v-e-r-y slowly, obviously on his last legs. After three weeks you should see nothing.

Boric acid is not toxic to adults, and accidentally swallowing a bit of it is not dangerous. A chemist in the Pesticide Regulation Division of the Federal Environmental Protection Agency said that in order for it to be harmful "a person would have to be trying to commit suicide. If you swallowed a pound of it, you'd be in trouble." Still, ordinary precautions should be taken to keep the dust out of areas where toddlers or pets might eat it. Although there are no vapors, self-appointed exterminators should also try not to inhale the powder during application. The material should not be applied to plants or soil that contains plants. Most plants have a low tolerance for the substance and soil contamination will severely burn or kill them.

Exterminators are gradually beginning to use boric acid, but Dr. C. Douglas Mampe, head of the New Jersey-based National Pest Control Association, estimates their number at about two out of 5,000 right now. "The association has no doubt of the efficacy of the powder," Dr. Mampe says, "but it works slowly and pest control men need something faster to make a dent in heavily-infested buildings."

THE CONVERSATION-PIECE CURES   If dusting does not appeal, there are a few last-ditch methods of control.

Get a tarantula. An enterprising Manhattan resident, who is also an assistant entomologist at the American Museum of Natural History, keeps a pet tarantula in his apartment just to get rid of roaches, a practice that is well known in the Antilles. Contrary to what is shown in the movies, tarantulas are really quite harmless to man, their bite a mere pin prick. The spider's venom can only kill something nearer its own size—say, of cockroach proportions.

The scientist keeps his pet in the bathroom, where he says she sometimes kills as many as two dozen roaches a day. A piece of string tied to the spider's two front legs and fastened at the other end to a paperweight keeps her from wandering away from her post just under the raised bathtub. Her owner leaves her a small dish filled with water to wash down her "lunch," and he scatters some bits of fruit around under the tub to attract the roaches (the spider is strictly carnivorous—doesn't touch the fruit). His roach population, he says, has dropped by about 50 percent.

Readers of—and writers for—New York's *Village Voice* weekly newspaper are everlastingly warring against the vile creatures ("you're lying in bed at night, and you know those bastards are out there, scrounging around for a toenail paring to dine on"), and they have come up with some equally offbeat killers. Like a gecko lizard. This brand of reptile ranges from five inches to a foot long and comes out only at night, same as the roaches. During the day he stays out of sight. Gecko lizards thrive on roaches. They can be tied to a bathtub or kitchen sink or, for the more adventurous, they can be allowed free rein in an apartment. They are relatively clean, too. Entomologists say they carry no more germs than any other living creature, man included. A $5 bill should get you one in decorator colors of purple, pink, and gray.

If the idea of a lizard climbing the walls seems too Tennessee Williams-ish, consider a Purple Pitcher Plant (Sarracenia purpura). It too thrives on cockroaches. A carnivorous green plant only a couple of inches high, it has bell-shaped "pitchers" which secrete a sweet substance that attracts the roaches. After munching their way a short distance into the pitchers, the insects quietly and aesthetically dissolve. No messy bodies to sweep up. Pitcher plants cost under $3. Lots of roaches? Buy several.

Rats

Cockroach stories can be bandied about with a touch of whimsy or black humor, but there is nothing funny about rats. Historically rats and mice have been the cause of more human illness and death than any other group of mammals. They carry many diseases: salmonellosis (food poisoning), trichinosis, the debilitating but not fatal leptospirosis and murine typhus fever and, what is probably the best known and most terrifying rat-caused pestilence, bubonic plague.

As threatening as they are to health, their effect on the spirit is more devastating. To low-income inner-city residents, rats represent all that is wrong with their environment. They are a cruel symbol of community degradation and neglect. Although rat bites are rarely fatal, they often leave mental and emotional scars that last far longer than the physical scars.

There is no accurate estimate of the rat population in the United States, although the figure of one rat for every person is often quoted. The United States Department of Health, Education and Welfare calculates that even if that figure is sliced in half, the country still has 100 million rats gnawing, contaminating and feeding on between $500 million and $1 billion worth of food and other materials *annually*.

"Domestic" rodents—Norway rats, roof rats, and house mice—gain entrance to a building in many ways. Especially attracted to deteriorating structures, they can come in through cracks in a building's foundation, holes around pipes or electrical inlets that enter the foundation or through holes in the floor around piping. Floor drains offer another exit from the underground. Outside, rats can be found rummaging through trash piles and open garbage cans.

Visible signs of a rodent population are tracks, gnawings in wood, droppings, greasy rubmarks along busy runways, and burrows along walls and under rubbish.

Traditionally, rat infestation has been associated with the poorest ghetto buildings. But they can be found in other types of housing too. If a structure next door to you is torn down, rat nests there are disturbed and the population may resettle in your building if access is easy. Areas around docks are susceptible. A buyer of an abandoned brownstone in a flourishing "new" neighborhood may find rats have long been in residence.

To eliminate the problem it is necessary to cut off their source of food. That means covering garbage tightly and in general keeping the premises clean. It also calls for closing necessary openings in an apartment house with wire mesh that rats cannot penetrate. Gaps in floors and walls should be sealed off at the landlord's expense.

Technically, your local health department or buildings department is responsible for rat clearance only in city-owned buildings and in parks, streets, subway stations, and so on. Privately owned apartment houses must pay for their own extermination programs, a system which on closer examination seems unfair since the city's rat control program should effectively keep the disease carriers out of residential buildings.

In some instances, however, the government has stepped in. In 1969 the Federal Urban Rat Control Program was initiated. It offered help with funding for extermination, personnel, and educational programs to local health departments and community organizations. To date thirty projects in twenty-nine cities have been conducted.

If there is a rat problem in your building, the landlord is responsible for getting rid of them. Rat infestation and large gaping holes in walls, ceilings, and floors from which they make their entrances into an apartment violate most housing codes and Board of Health statutes. If you get no satisfaction from the landlord, contact these two offices directly and they will get after him. In some instances, rent strikes have been called until a landlord provided extermination.

Although do-it-yourself poisons and traps are available at supermarkets and hardware stores, a rat problem is serious enough to pass up fiddling around on your own and get professional help. If you do decide to use poisons as a followup to an extermination "clean out," or as a preventive measure, be careful which ones you choose. Some are dangerous indoors and are best suited for use around wood piles and outside trash cans.

The most effective rodenticides are the anticoagulants (warfarin, Fumarin and Pival), fortified red squill and, to a lesser extent, ANTU.

Another advantage to initial professional treatment is that an exterminator will be able to identify the breed of rat in your building, which will help you in purchasing the proper poisons later.

If for some reason you are paying the exterminator yourselves, you should know that the "clean out" process for rats is less expensive than for cockroaches. Dr. C. Douglas Mampe, head of the National Pest Control Association, explains that the cockroach job involves treating individual apartment units, whereas rodent treatment is confined to the exterior and basement of the building.

Other riffraff

Although not as serious a problem as cockroaches and rats, there are still other more mundane household pests that drive homeowners and tenants frantic.

PANTRY PESTS (WEEVILS, BEETLES) These insects infest flour, cereals, and other dry foods. Wash shelves thoroughly with a mixture of chlordane and water and then spray with a commercial aerosol bomb. Sprays work very well with the smaller, easier-to-kill pests. Do not spray, however, if you have roaches besides. If you have both, poor soul, you will kill the weevils but bring out the roaches. All foods that come in bags and boxes should be transferred to tight-lidded jars or canisters. You will no doubt want to throw out any insect-infested food, but one entomologist says there is no need. You can destroy the insects, he says, by heating the dry foods in the oven for half an hour at 140°. This seems overly economical, though, even in penny-squeezing times.

SILVERFISH Dark brown bugs about a half inch in length, these pests like undisturbed areas such as basements or attics. They are seldom found in living areas, although they can crop up in long unopened trunks or boxes of stored books. They feed on wallpaper, books and other starchy materials. Wash the affected areas and spray with a supermarket pesticide.

MOTHS These familiar troublemakers feed on anything that contains wool, down, mohair or feathers. They are carried indoors on clothing in almost invisible eggs that develop into larvae. They will mate, reproduce and die without leaving your closet or bureau drawer. Clothes moths are a different species than the ones you see flying around outside or circling your lamps at night. To keep clothes moth-free, spread mothballs or flakes around closet shelves and in drawers where clothing is stored in the spring and fall. Apartment dwellers may have a problem here in airing winter clothes once the frost is on the pumpkin. If they still smell of moth flakes after hanging them in the apartment for several days, next season try packing smaller items—scarves, sweaters, caps—in individual plastic sweater or garment bags with no moth flakes. All openings around the bags *must* be sealed off with tape, however, if the clothes are to be safe from moth penetration.

BEDBUGS Oval-shaped, quarter-inch-long brown bugs, these pests are brought into a residence through infested pieces of overstuffed furniture—mattresses, sofas, upholstered chairs. The furniture is almost always second-hand, never new. Many of the better second-hand furniture stores routinely treat their merchandise for bedbugs, but if you do bring home an item that shows signs of life, spray it and the entire wall and floor surface around it with an ordinary pesticide.

CARPET BEETLES Sometimes confused with clothes moths because they both do pretty much the same damage and also feed on woolens. They lay eggs that hatch into the small, fuzzy brown larvae we recognize so well. But carpet beetles can also live on hair, lint and other organic matter that collects in corners, around baseboards and other frequently neglected spots. A thorough cleansing of the area, followed by a pesticide, will see them disappear.

Unlike cockroaches, once you manage to get rid of the pests mentioned above, you are rid of them for good. If you prefer extermination to your own efforts, an exterminator can treat your apartment for rats, cockroaches and any other invaders all on the same routine contract call. Do tell him first, though, just what and where your problems are so he will know what he is gunning for.

ANTS are not, according to Dr. Mampe, a problem in apartment buildings. But if they are crawling up the side of the private home in which you are a first-floor tenant, you can stop the march by spraying around the window and door frames, the patio landing and the sides of the building up to window level. If they are as far as the kitchen floor, or in wall cabinets, wash the area and spray. Baits work too for certain kinds of ants. But if yours are the type that nest within the building's partitions, it may be impossible to locate the nest in order to flush them out. If infestation persists despite your scouring, you will need an exterminator.

PALMETTOS   A type of cockroach found in the south, this bug prefers the outdoors—palm trees and other tropical shrubs, to be exact—and will only move inside if the weather is very dry or cool. At such times a single-family homeowner may find a handful of palmettos (and at one and a half inches long that's quite a handful!) in his living room, but apartment dwellers, unless they live on a ground floor, are not usually troubled by the bugs. If they do show up, spraying with a pesticide should get rid of them. Unlike the ordinary household roach, once the palmetto is gone, he's gone.

TERMITES are not an apartment problem either. For the record, these crawlers usually live in nests in the soil and must maintain contact between the moisture of the soil and the wood of the house they are busily chomping at. Termite exterminators operate on the principle of breaking that contact.

If you are harboring a *genus curious* that does not fit into any of the above categories, the United States government may be able to help sweep it away. Send the insect in an envelope or other container to Insect Identification, Agricultural Research Service, ARC West, Beltsville, Maryland 20705. Indicate if you can where the insect was found. They will identify it and advise you on how to get rid of it.

CHAPTER 9

□

Tenant Organizing

It's time to add to "black power" and "women's liberation" another movement that is determined to ruffle the tranquility of the status quo: tenant power.

Since discovering the power of organization and numbers, tenants have become a force to be reckoned with, not only in confrontations with landlords, but in courtrooms and legislative corridors as well. Their mobilization has taken the form of small, individual building unions, larger neighborhood and community associations, and statewide coalitions. In California and New York there are even tenants' parties with special slates of candidates. Nationwide, the National Tenants Organization, representing all renters, has helped thousands of apartment dwellers toward improved living conditions, particularly those in public housing projects.

What do tenants want? Some unions are formed for social purposes, but in the majority of buildings the catalyst for organizing is poor housing conditions and the futility experienced in trying to right them. What tenants generally want, therefore, is: 1) to see the nature of the landlord–tenant relationship revised to make rights and responsibilities for both parties more equitable and 2) to establish ongoing collective bargaining agreements with landlords where the groups are recognized as tenant councils and bargaining units. (Such groups also want the right to bring in an arbitrator when the situation warrants one.)

The tenant movement as we know it today (there was an earlier, brief flare-up in the 1930s protesting economic conditions of the time) was spawned in the ferment of the mid-1960s, much of it linked with the black struggle. Young, radical lawyers and activists representing the cause of the inner-city poor saw bad housing as a major villain in the ghettoes, and bad housing equaled bad landlords. Rent strikes and other pressure tactics were utilized—many of them successfully—to correct conditions. At the very least they set an example for future warring tenants by showing them that collective action can work.

It was originally a movement of and for the poor, but as vacancy levels in the larger cities shrank, mobilization spread to high-rent buildings, and it became not unusual to see banners proclaiming a rent strike streaming from the plushest apartment windows. One tenant could not hope to gain the landlord's ear, let alone upset the balance of power. But a united, determined building could—just as the single worker can be ignored but the labor union must be heard.

The specific grievances of the tenants' groups in the last ten years fall into four principal areas: 1) arbitrary rent increases; 2) bad housing conditions, where buildings often have many code violations; 3) poor security, and 4) the owner's plan to convert to a cooperative or condominium.

Gains have been impressive. On a one-building-to-one-landlord basis the nation's hundreds of tenant unions have won thousands of awards from owners or, failing that, from the courts. They range from structural repairs to better locks on apartment doors to damage suits to the right to organize without fear of reprisals.

Larger, statewide legislation is being promulgated, offering even better protection. Some recent tenant-agitated laws include:

• In Maryland what is believed to be the nation's first statewide rent control law was signed in 1973. Thanks to the persistence of the New Jersey Tenants Organization, more than 80 communities in that state now have "rent leveling" strictures, limiting rent increases to a formula based on rises in the Consumer Price Index. (Hundreds of communities in the country now have some form of rent legislation.)

• The New Jersey Tenants Organization in 1973 saw the passage of a bill regulating security deposits. Landlords in that state must notify a tenant where security money is deposited and must return the deposit within 30 days after the tenant has moved out or furnish adequate reasons for not returning it. Otherwise the tenant is entitled to double his deposit. (Again, bills regulating security deposits, although not identical to New Jersey's, are in effect locally.)

• Arizona and Washington states have adopted the Model Landlord-Tenant Law of the National Conference of Commissioners on Uniform State Laws, a document which greatly toughens landlord obligations. California, Ohio, Oregon, Illinois and Wisconsin are considering the bill. Other states might follow, although the bill will have a tough time of it in New York, Massachusetts and possibly Connecticut—populous areas where it is badly needed, but where tenant lobbying is weaker than that of landlords.

• The Oregon Consumer League, one of the most active consumer groups in the nation, has successfully fought for improved landlord–tenant legislation in several areas, notably in a law which prohibits a landlord from access to an apartment without two days' notice, except in an emergency, and in laws which prohibit retaliatory evictions and regulate security deposits. They aren't resting on their successes either. More bills are pending.

• In California, tenants' rights bills are being run off at a steady clip. Under California law tenants can now use the kind of deduction previously allotted only to homeowners and can reduce their taxes by as much as $45. The state already forbids retaliatory evictions for reporting housing violations, allows tenants to deduct repairs from rent money in certain circumstances and, early in 1974, the state Supreme Court granted legal protection to tenants who refuse to pay rent in protest against a landlord's failure to make adequate building repairs.

Yes, tenants agree that the laws are changing. But they hasten to add that much more work remains to be done. All tenants' attitudes must be lifted from an ingrained subjugation and sense of futility to a new self-esteem and awareness of their—*anyone's* —right to decent housing at a decent rent. The education process must extend to judges who automatically rubber stamp landlord causes in court and legislators who, while realizing that far more of their constituents are tenants than building owners, still see landlords as an enormous power bloc.

Another consideration that may hold up mass tenant awareness and subsequent plans for action is that some parts of the country appear to be at peace in the rental relationship and cannot be counted on for support in presenting a nationwide image of aroused tenants—at least not until many a consciousness has been raised. There is little, if any, tenant activity in Los Angeles or Miami, for instance. Renters caught in a bad situation in those cities will switch rather than fight. And with a reasonable vacancy rate in both places it is possible to play musical apartments. But in densely populated cities such as New York, Washington, D.C., San Francisco and clogged university towns such as Berkeley, California and Ann Arbor, Michigan, where vacancy levels can run as low as 1 percent, tenants cannot look elsewhere for housing. They have to stay.

And they usually elect to fight. Attacks have taken the form of harassing the landlord and local rent and housing agencies, lobbying at state capitols, testing the courts, and working quietly on new proposals for the lawmakers.

It should be pointed out in this chapter that although this book necessarily concentrates on landlord–tenant conflicts, there are many good landlords. Their property is well maintained, repairs are made promptly, and if their financial situation precludes any extra sprucing up, at least tenants are informed why. The lines of communication are open. There may be griping behind those polite discussions, but basically the relationship is . . . well, not bad.

Landlords are eager to point out that they have problems, too. They say tenants don't understand the economics of housing. Building owners are also victims: They must cope with bad tenants who destroy the building and/or skip without paying rent, with rising taxes and maintenance costs and a continually growing demand for additional services.

Building owners also feel that many tenant groups hold a leftist-socialist philosophy that directly contradicts the landlord's belief in private ownership. This belief on the part of the landlords makes negotiations especially difficult.

When tenant associations do launch a mass attack, landlord responses vary. Some agree to such reasonable demands as fixing housing code violations; others hold off until the collective actions reach the point of an income-withholding rent strike; still others will not talk at all to tenant unions.

William D. Sally, vice president of a Chicago real estate firm, writing in *The National Real Estate Investor,* a trade publication, suggests to other realty people that one way to deal with the problems of taking over an existing building with demanding tenants and previously poor management "is to cancel all existing leases. This then gives you the chance to screen all the present tenants and deny lease renewals to the undesirable ones. . . . We did this recently when we took over the management of a . . . development that was undergoing extensive renovation. It was necessary to move people out of the buildings as the renovation proceeded in phases. We offered the desirable tenants quarters in other buildings until their new apartments were ready; the less desirable tenants were denied new leases." Not a new strategy, ridding a complex of dissidents. It is a suggestion that has long been made at courses in apartment management.

Mr. Sally goes on to say his company's policy is to "negotiate with individuals, never with groups. . . . Negotiating with groups, we've found, is dangerous. Not only is the group unwieldy to deal with and apt to become a mob rather than a committee, but many times the group is under the sway of a leader who has his own desires to satisfy."

Management-instituted tenant groups

Attempting to stave off the organization of potentially troublesome unions in their building, a growing number of building owners are taking the initiative in bringing landlord and tenant to the discussion table. *They* are setting up the tenant associations. The councils can work in several ways. Two or three residents can represent the tenants on a management governing board, bringing suggestions and grievances to the board's attention, but having little or no voting power on their implementation. Or, more likely, tenant associations are set up initially by management and then turned over completely to the tenants. This form is better from the tenants' view, of course, in that the group functions autonomously. Management usually picks the spot for the first meeting and probably provides coffee and cake. Perhaps they offer a few hundred dollars for a newsletter. Sometimes they are represented at all future meetings.

Whatever the practical/altruistic ratio in organizing tenants, the management that starts a tenant association is to be commended. The tenants get to know one another, they realize the strength of their numbers, and problems and potential trouble spots can be discussed with building owners before they explode under the compression of a long buildup.

Management-sponsored tenant associations are more likely to be instituted in new, garden-type communities where everything is shiny new and functioning beautifully. No landlord is going to get things stirred up in an older building or complex where problems may already be evident and tenants ripe for action. The organizations are also an effective sales tool in areas with a high vacancy rate and keen competition for renters. In those cases the association is likely to be touted for its social program. Here is how two such organizations function:

About half the residents of a new, sixty-two-unit townhouse community in Brooklyn, N.Y., attend meetings of the RAC Gardens Tenant Association, conceived by The New York Urban Coalition. Some of the group's discussions include: procedures for paying rent each month; why the "no pets" rule; the possibility of converting the rental apartments into a cooperative some time in the future; a decision to order picket fences for the front yards (each family paying for its own fence); and alarm systems (what they cost and which kind would be best). The association has started collecting monthly dues which will go toward the purchase of a mimeograph machine for running off flyers and a monthly newsletter. The money will also be used for an entertainment program.

In Lafayette, Ind., the residents of the 326-unit Westchester Estates are equally involved with the workings of their complex. And if the tenants seem younger than the usual apartment mix, it is because many of them are students at nearby Purdue University. The development was built and is managed by Cloverleaf Development Corporation.

When the development opened in 1971, Cloverleaf tried to stir up interest in a residents' group by instituting a summer camp for the tenants' children. Only fifteen children participated. That fall management called the first residents' meeting. Twelve persons attended—again, not much of a turnout. But those tenants *were* interested in the complex, and they served as a strong nucleus for the development of the association to its present strength.

The Cloverleaf management rarely attends tenant meetings, but it does have a management representative who does. Some of the association's accomplishments: additional bus stops around the project; the design of a new playground at the common area by a design class at Purdue, with area merchants supplying materials. The council recently asked Cloverleaf to purchase an acre of land adjacent to Westchester Estates. The additional land was subdivided into small plots and leased to tenants for a small fee for use as a vegetable garden. The council also successfully petitioned management to build a fence along a portion of the complex which ran along a busy street.

How to start your own building tenant association

You don't need a problem to galvanize your fellow tenants. But the demon apathy being what it is, that is how most building tenant unions begin. Rumor of a rent increase is circulated, or mounting repairs are unmade long past the statute of limitations. Sometimes, following a spate of burglaries or muggings, tenants band together in seeking better building security. Whatever the reason for organizing, a few ringleaders decide on a tenants' meeting and spread the word to other residents in the building.

Attendance at that first meeting will probably be good, but it may not hold up. Much of that initial enthusiasm will merely be curiosity. At the next meeting there will be fewer faces and at the one after that too. Some of this fall-off will no doubt be due to fear of reprisals. But interest will pick up again after the organization has won one, even small, victory, and the tenants see that you mean business.

The tone of the first meeting should be informal. It is principally a getting-acquainted session. Organizers can introduce the problems in the building and explain what the aims of the group will be. Anyone who wants to should be allowed to speak, even though heads may nod at the droning "and then on November 4 I sent a letter. . . ." Hearing everyone out is only fair. Besides, you may find some additional points to add to your presentation.

Whatever else you are all fighting for, a collective bargaining agreement should be included in any list of tenant demands. The agreement is vital to the peaceful settlement of any future problems, for ongoing communication with the landlord and for formal recognition of the gains your group has made. It can be drawn up by your lawyer and filed in a city or county office. It should be in effect for any new owners of the building. See page 172 in this chapter for a list of tenant awards in the bargaining pact for a small Philadelphia building. It should provide some ideas for your union.

If there is time at the first meeting for election of officers, you will need a president, vice-president, secretary, and treasurer. You will also need individuals or committees to handle the following: publicity (contact with the media); finances; drafting the letter or resolution to the landlord and working with it (and him) to conclusion; in-house contact (announcing meeting dates or sending around flyers). Don't make an empire-building production of organizing, however. And no cliques either. Elected officers should be spread fairly among all the tenants. What a good organization needs most is hard-working, tenacious officers who will make a favorable impression in negotiating with management and talking to the media and others useful to your purpose.

The type of people you elect to represent you and their method of operation can make or break your organization. It is understandable that you are all brimming over with indignation at the very real injustices in your building or with landlord–tenant law in general. Any fair-minded person will sympathize with your cause. Don't let venom make you shrill and hysterical in talking with local elected officials or the press or even with building management. It is only human nature to want to shut off anyone—no matter how just his cause—who has not bothered to inform himself properly of the immediate facts at issue and the larger picture, and who just will not shut up and listen for a moment. Like all new movements whose members are exploding in long-bottled-up violent rhetoric, tenants can find themselves turning off just the people they need. They become "those crazies from Belmont Street." If your "front people" are knowledgeable, reasonable and even pleasant to talk to, that does not mean they have to be any less aggressive or persistent than it takes to get the job done. Consider their personality just one more tactic that must be employed in order to get what you want.

Off the soapbox and back to the first few meetings. Leaders of the group should collect in advance printed material from the citywide or statewide tenant associations to pass out to attendees. It is even better if possible to have a member of one of those groups at your meeting. If you live in a community that has not been awakened to the tenant movement, you will probably have to retain a lawyer if you are planning to file suit or if you feel you are headed toward a rent strike. Otherwise you won't need one right away. Try to get one who is familiar with real estate law. It's a complicated field and lawyers whose specialities are in other areas can often be just as confused as you are about ever-changing landlord–tenant laws. Remember, though, that the lawyer is there for counsel, not decision making. And never let the case so completely out of your hands that it becomes a your-lawyer–their-lawyer discussion, with the lawyers making the decisions.

If there is a savvy tenant organization in your area, you can probably manage without a lawyer. They can see you through your battles, even guiding you through a rent strike. But you need one or the other. Tenants new to militancy are finding there are many landmines out there. Counsel of some sort is vital.

With officers and committees set and major aims outlined, your next order of business is to give yourselves a name. Then you can turn your attention to the landlord. If you don't know who he is (a point that will be corrected in the Model Landlord–Tenant Code—landlords will be required to disclose their correct business name to renters), your lawyer or an appointed tenant can find out by checking the local tax assessor's office. Or, if the building is large and/or well-known in the community, the reporter who covers that area for your local paper might help. Title insurance companies also have information about the ownership of property because they handle mortgages and so forth. You may have to pay a fee for their services, although your lawyer probably will not.

If your complaint is in the area of building repairs, follow the above bit of detection with a check of housing code violations on the building. Here again a lawyer will probably have better access to these facts than a lone tenant will, but it might be possible to enlist the help of a sympathetic city employee. See when the building was last inspected and whether the violations were corrected. Have there been any complaints registered by tenants? If there are no violations, that may take a little wind out of your sails; you will have nothing with which to threaten the landlord, and your group may lose interest. If a new inspection can be made, you might get a more up-to-date list of what's wrong. Before you use that list as a weapon, however, make sure that the conditions were due to landlord negligence—not caused by the tenants. Bear in mind, too, that if the place is really in bad shape, you run the risk of the city closing it and declaring it uninhabitable. Another problem, particularly in low-income buildings, is that once the landlord makes repairs and charges a fair rent, there will probably be no way he can make a profit, except perhaps through tax consideration. Maybe he will be forced to walk away from his property. If that should happen, would you be ready to consider taking over the building yourselves?

Tactics

Once everyone is heard out and a list of grievances drawn up, you are ready to approach the landlord. Send him by mail the demand(s) of the new tenant association. Allow him two weeks to reply. If he decides to talk with the organization, be sure it is indeed the owner you are meeting with, or at least someone in a position to make decisions. Corporations holding apartment projects sometimes send their public relations people to talk to dissidents. Have none of that. And meet in your building or on some neutral territory, not in the landlord's office.

Management may surprise you by giving in to demands right

away, perhaps even making one or two repairs on your list. But then, nothing. They are hoping the group will disband and indeed at this point many of them do. In any long-running battle (and these conflicts tend to last at least one month longer than everyone's patience), the greatest danger is that the tenant union will not hold together. Management spots the weakness and takes advantage of it. So present a strong and united front, no matter how much squabbling and indecision goes on behind the scene.

Should the landlord totally ignore the union, you can take the following steps:

1) You can, depending on the nature of your complaint, file a lawsuit.

2) You can try harassment to get his attention: Pass out flyers or picket his office or home. Picketing the apartment building won't be effective if the owner never goes near the place, but it might attract the attention of the media. It certainly will if your publicity people contact them (see "utilizing the media" in Chapter 12, "Where to Complain").

3) If it is building repairs you are seeking, you can make them yourselves and deduct the money from rent. But check your local rent office before attempting this strategy. Where it is allowed at all, there are qualifications galore.

4) You can threaten the landlord with a rent strike to gain his attention. But hold off actually starting one as long as you can. Rent strikes are costly in time, money, energy, and emotions.

Rent strikes

A continued, mass rent-withholding—the rent strike—is probably the tenants' most dramatic weapon against the landlord who won't listen.

Legally, withholding rent is grounds for eviction or a lawsuit, but in some states strikes can be carried on within the law if they follow certain guidelines. In other instances they have been carried on *outside* the law, again following a prescribed form. Usually tenants must be protesting conditions that make the building uninhabitable—dangers to safety and health. No plumbing, for instance, not that everyone needs more parking spaces. Rents must be deposited into a special escrow account until the strike is settled. The fund is controlled by the tenants, or by the courts or by some outside agency. In the case of a protest against a rent increase, the amount of the proposed increase is held in escrow; tenants pay the original rent to the landlord as usual. Naturally escrow balances will be closely monitored by the tenants.

Landlords point out that rent strikes contribute to building decay and eventual abandonment by tying up rents in escrow funds for months and depriving owners of money for repairs. If the landlords are so eager to make repairs, tenants retort, why didn't they do so before the strike became necessary? Sometimes landlords say they can't make repairs without raising rents. Tenants reply they can barely afford present rent scales. There, sad to say, both sides are sometimes right.

The following is an account of one building's rent action:

It had been raining for days in Philadelphia that September. It was raining in Beverly and Van Jones's bedroom, too. The rug was wet from seepage, attracting mildew which began creeping up the walls. Books belonging to Mrs. Jones, a teacher, were ruined. So were her paintings. Notebooks of her husband's poetry were also destroyed. Dresser drawers began sticking. Worst of all was the terrible odor that permeated the room. It got into the couple's clothes, resulting in huge cleaning bills. The condition of the room became so bad it was necessary to close it off entirely.

Mrs. Jones complained to the landlord, but got no response. The rental agent for the building, which is a two-story brick structure in the Germantown section of the city, told her if she didn't like conditions there she could move out. Pleas for help to the housing department were equally fruitless. A ruined rug, Mrs. Jones was told, did not constitute an unfit living condition.

The Joneses could have moved, but they liked Greene Street and had many friends in the building and in the neighborhood. Racking her brain for where to turn next, Mrs. Jones recalled a tenant association in the area which had helped other renters. She called them.

The Northwest Tenants Organization has won several impressive victories in the northwest section of Philadelphia where it operates. In particular, it has helped secure collective bargaining agreements for nine of the twenty buildings it represents. Almost all the agreements were won as concessions following a rent strike. Rudy Tolbert, executive director of NWTO, explains that the dual goal of his organization, a federation of tenant unions in operation since 1967, is the organization of tenants in their respective buildings and the procurement of collective bargaining agreements for them. He is emphatic about the need for the latter in balancing landlord power.

Mr. Tolbert asked if any of the other tenants in the 14-unit building had complaints. Mrs. Jones wasn't certain so she called a tenants' meeting to find out. Naturally, once the question was asked, a Pandora's box of gripes was aired. There were leaky faucets, bad caulking jobs, dirty hallways and windows in the common areas. The latter was especially irksome since part of the rent payments were to go to the salary of a superintendent.

Mr. Tolbert decided the building was ripe for collective action. It was basically a sound structure, the tenantry was small, knew one another and were already mobilized. With the encouragement of the NWTO leader the tenants wrote the landlord asking for a meeting. If they didn't have the meeting before the next month's rent was due, there would be no next month's rent.

The deadline came and no word from management. So the rent strike began. Constable notices appeared on all fourteen doors, but were quickly torn down after NWTO informed the landlord that they had been delivered illegally. Another month went by. Then the striking house gained unexpected support. Tenants discovered that two other buildings in the area were owned by the same man. Residents from all three dwellings met and compared complaints. Another letter to the landlord, this time from the other two buildings calling for meetings. "All right," replied the landlord, "we'll meet with one of you." "Uh-uh, all or none," said the tenants. The landlord agreed at last to meet with spokespeople from all three houses. Nothing was accomplished, but then the meeting lasted only twenty minutes. Now all three buildings were on rent strike, with the threat of eviction hovering over their collective heads.

By this time Beverly Jones, who was now president of the Greene St. West Tenants Union, noticed strangers around the building. They turned out to be prospective buyers for the property. When they were apprised of the conflict with the present owner by Mrs. Jones, they agreed to sit in on negotiations. Far more amenable than the previous owner, the new owners wrapped up an agreement with the tenants in six meetings within one month. The Greene St. tenants (and residents of the other two striking buildings) won one-and-one-half-year bargaining agreements which awarded the tenants 1) the right to examine the landlord's books and records pertaining to the costs of operating the building; 2) the right to repair certain damages, deducting the cost from rent; 3) the right to arbitration in the case of unsettled disputes; 4) the right to screen prospective tenants; 5) the right to repair schedules for damages. For their part, tenants agreed to keep up their individual units, to pay rent promptly and to abide by municipal code regulations governing overcrowding of units.

Since the pact was signed, Mrs. Jones reports few problems with management. For a while the building had a do-nothing superintendent, and a few tenants were rented apartments without the agreed-upon screening process. But the early shakedown period is over now and the system is working effectively. Rent increases may be a problem at renegotiation time, but overall the small building on Greene Street is faring far better than many another multiple dwelling in the nation.

Some other successful rent strikes, capsulized:

• A strike conducted by tenants in a high-rent building in New York City facing Gramercy Park. It lasted four months. Tenant complaints: blistered plaster walls, the result of defective plumbing; windows that could not be opened; rotting window sills; dimly lighted hallways; wires dangling from unused electrical connections; and a drunken doorman. The judge ruled the first two months' rent were to be paid to the building's owner for repairs, while the next two months' rent (and if need be any future rents) were to be paid into an escrow fund until those repairs were made.

• A 1968 rent strike by tenants in a public housing project in Muskegon Heights, Michigan, resulted in the residents obtaining a voice in the selection of a majority of the public housing authority. The tenants also won a recognition of their organization, a new rent scale, grievance procedures and an agreement on building repairs.

• Tenants in the Hudson Towers in New York City won a collective bargaining agreement and $47,000 in much-needed repairs to the five buildings that comprise the project. All eighty apartments received new mortise locks, chain locks and peep holes. A buzzer, an intercom system, and new glass and steel outside doors were installed in all the buildings. Painting was done and repairs were made to the roof. All housing violations— and there were 300 of them—were corrected.

• A victory in New Jersey saw tenants at the new Colony Apartments, a super-luxury high-rise along the Hudson River in Fort Lee, win an eight-week rent strike conducted for amenities the developer had promised but never delivered: a community room, air-conditioned bus service to Manhattan, additional storage space, and a bicycle room.

Most, but not all, rent strikes end either with outright victory for tenants or at least with acceptable compromises. But there are defeats. A rent strike in Berkeley, California, in the late 1960s led to the establishment of a rent board in that community and a rent control program. But in 1973 Alameda County Court Judge Robert L. Bostick ruled the rent control law unconstitutional, citing that there is a question that the housing emergency, upon which the law was based, actually exists. The Berkeley Fair Rent Committee, the tenant group that framed the measure and worked for its passage, claims that with vacancy levels at 3 percent, a rent rise of 60 percent in the years from 1960 to 1970, and no new construction planned, there is indeed a housing emergency. The decision is under appeal, but in the meantime rent curbs have been lifted, and naturally rents are again spiraling.

Other activities of a tenant union

After your organization's demands have been met, by peaceful negotiation or rent strike, and the relationship with the landlord is back on a more or less even keel, do not disband the tenant association. It is now a working, viable structure. Keep it going with long-range goals and plans. If you've succeeded in obtaining a collective bargaining agreement, it is that much more important that you remain in force.

Tenant associations can function in peace as well as war. Unions around the country are operating food-buying clubs, babysitting co-ops, day-care centers, and credit unions. Security-wise, a building organization can organize tenant patrols around the complex or on the block. You can purchase a marking kit and set about identifying all your property against theft. Look into social programs, too—chartering buses for day trips and perhaps even a plane for long-distance discount jaunts. Actually, by your organization and numbers you present a stabilizing influence in the neighborhood and can effect some positive changes in many different areas. For example, you can plant trees or buy sodium lights for better protection on the streets. To raise money for yourselves or for a neighborhood project you can put together a block fair or a covered dish supper or a roof party. In East St. Louis, Illinois, the tenants in one large project run a cooperative laundry financed by a Small Business Administration grant. After the debt is paid off, proceeds will go for tuition for tenants in a beauty school course. Tenants in turn will set up a co-op beauty shop in the complex. A San Francisco building for the elderly has established a "buddy" system, where residents check in on one another when ill. A somewhat similar program is operating in a New York tower's Human Help Bank, where tenants take turns being "on call" to help other residents in the house with housekeeping or personal problems. In a Boston project, tenants have established a closed-circuit radio station from which they broadcast local news.

As you see, it is immaterial here how much or how little money is in your treasury. A tenant organization's activity is limited only by its members' imagination and enthusiasm.

CHAPTER 10

☐

How to Publish a Newsletter

At an increasing number of apartment buildings these days the tie that binds is a monthly newsletter. Whether casually typed on a machine that needs cleaning, or professionally produced with the embellishments of paid advertising, a house bulletin is a warm touch to what is too often the cold anonymity of apartment life.

Newsletters serve several purposes. On the purely social level, they can introduce tenants to one another in print before they have a chance to meet in person, making it easier to seek out those one would like to know better. A blessing for the shy or newly-moved-in tenant. And, operating on the "strength in numbers" principle, a house organ can exercise a little clout in getting necessary repairs and changes made in an apartment building. Tenants do not realize their power until they organize, and one of the more pleasant initial ways of banding together is to get acquainted with one another via the newsletter. In a very large complex of several hundred or more units, a newsletter is a must if information is to be properly disseminated, especially if the residents have already formed a tenants' group.

Is there an editor in the house?

Talking up the idea for the paper is easy. Everyone will be enthusiastic—as long as someone else does the work. As with most ventures of this sort, the one who gets the idea is usually elected to see it through. If that person is you, don't worry; it isn't a difficult job. All the editors quoted in this chapter appear to be enjoying themselves immensely. Publishing what amounts to your own newspaper is, when you think of it, a pretty rare volunteer job (yes, unfortunately, *volunteer*). You can set your own hours and operate from your living room. It is independent and creative work, with the satisfaction of seeing an idea right through to the finished product, a product that will almost certainly enhance the quality of life in your building and no doubt the neighborhood as well. Involvement beyond your own walls is inevitable. "If we want to improve our building," one editor says, "we've got to improve the neighborhood too. You cannot isolate yourselves from the community."

No journalism background is needed to write the paper. Since space will be limited, getting the message across in simple English, without flights of vivid writing, is probably all there will be room for. Building newspapers usually do not have photographs or elaborate artwork so no special graphics talent is necessary either. Time-wise you can expect to spend three or four hours a month on your work.

And an editor need not be the village gossip to keep the news columns filled. On the contrary, you will uncover an old publishing secret rather early in the game: people love to see their names in print. Remember "I don't care what you say about me, as long as you spell my name correctly"? Keep after fellow tenants to fill you in on anything newsworthy happening in their lives until they do so automatically. No doubt, besides the legitimate news tips, you will be awash in non-stories and dreadful poems—but then a surfeit of copy does make an editor feel secure! Once the paper gets underway you may find a cohort who can serve as a "reporter," covering a wing of the building you do not often visit or social events you cannot always attend.

An editor must be aware of all that goes on under his roof, from dates of tenants' meetings to an explanation of why management still has not fixed that out-of-order elevator. He should also have a good relationship with his neighbors. "They call *me* with their problems," one editor says of his readers. "I guess it's because my name is on the newsletter and I'm the only one they feel they can turn to." Finally editors should maintain a pleasant—and reasonably objective—relationship with management to be able to talk with them about new policies and physical changes in the building that should be carried in the paper.

Does the well of story ideas ever run dry? The part-time journalists almost unanimously say no. A lone exception admitted that seemingly nightmarish vacuum of having no news to print has occurred, but on those occasions the paper simply does not come out that month. If it is January that is skimpy with news, the next issue will be dated January–February. This problem arises more often in small buildings with a limited or non-existent social program. Harvey A. Becker, recreational director (and newsletter editor) for four apartment complexes operated by the Gross Realty & Construction Company in scattered suburban Philadelphia locations, gets around a news shortage by using "fillers" culled from magazines and newspapers. For example, he might run a general how-to information article—such as a few paragraphs on the best way to clean venetian blinds. At another location in the same apartment complexes, the newsletter is printed by hand to make it appear longer.

News content

Here are some copy suggestions:

  • New tenants—a sentence or two introducing newcomers to the building. Management can supply their names;

• Interviews with employees and tenants having unusual jobs or backgrounds;

• An explanation of physical changes underway in the building or new policies handed down by management;

• Letters to the editor;

• Classified advertising—merchandise for sale, babysitting and dogwalking services, and so on. If the paper is non-profit, there is no charge to tenants placing the ads;

• Poetry by tenants, even the very young ones;

• Helpful tips and recommendations. A sentence or two, for instance, about a tenant who found a good carpenter to build and install his bookshelves;

• In cooperatives and condominiums, reports from the board of managers; in rental buildings, minutes of tenants' meetings;

• A calendar of upcoming events in the building;

• Back-fence news—who's in the hospital, who's home from vacation, wedding notes and obituaries.

Let's look at some specific papers, to see how three newsletter editors fill their columns. Each has a slightly different approach. In fact, funding for the three periodicals is different, which has more than a little to do with their respective styles.

The "Homestead Manor Newsletter" is a management-run service for the residents of a 68-unit, rental garden complex in Dallas, Texas. It is a small but active enclave, and its monthly bulletin is full of newsy items about chili suppers and poolside sales and bay window decorating contests at Christmas. The only cloud over that almost perpetual sunshine is an occasional caution that outsiders are not allowed to use the pool or a complaint that residents of the next apartment community are using Homestead Manor's trash cans. The news sheet is written by the development's resident manager although the tenants do, of course, supply her with many of the news tips.

Taking a completely different editorial tack is "The Bulletin Board," a somewhat militant newsletter edited by the tenants' council of the Dorchester Towers, a rental building in New York City. The council is extremely active, and its newspaper, which is paid for by tenant subscriptions, reflects the group's intense concern for better living conditions both in the building and the surrounding West Side neighborhood, an area of luxury high-rise dwellings, shops, tenements, restored brownstones and squalid hotels.

Hans Reinisch, who for five years was president of the tenants' council and is now president emeritus, says the paper was instituted after management removed from a bulletin board in the building several notices by tenants seeking to organize. That is why the paper is called "The Bulletin Board."

It appears there is nothing this enterprising staff will not tackle. In one November issue alone, the four-page paper

    • congratulated itself on getting management to put a lock on the side door of the building;

    • complained that the local supermarket raised milk prices 1¢ a quart and increased delivery charges by 100 percent;

    • clarified a clause in tenants' leases after advice from the New York City Rent Stabilization Association;

    • reminded tenants "it is a violation of law to offer tips to federal, state or city employees [at Christmas] and it is also a violation of the law for them to accept such gifts";

    • printed fifteen excerpts from letters to the editor complaining about building security following removal of the phone from the lobby desk, where tenants could make outside calls, and management's directive that the building's side door must be used by those with baby carriages, dogs, and shopping carts;

    • announced the formation of the Human Help Bank where residents would take turns being "on call" to help other tenants in the house with a variety of housekeeping or personal problems;

    • requested tenants to keep doors closed when cooking;

    • published results of a presidential election poll and ballot propositions taken among residents.

The remainder of that particular issue of "The Bulletin Board" featured a few classified ads, a calendar of events, and one poem.

Another paper is distributed a few blocks north of the Dorchester Towers in a 15-story cooperative building. Barbara Sussman, editor of the "250 House Letter" ("250" is the address), which is paid for with funds allotted by the board of directors, says she prefers to stay away from topics that do not directly affect the co-op owners in her building. That means no zoning battles or school disputes or anything political. As she puts it: "My newsletter is the only thing the residents read these days that isn't controversial, and they like it that way."

Ms. Sussman's editorial stance is somewhere between the Homestead Manor and Dorchester Towers papers. Besides publishing chit-chat, she does do some hard news reporting. After hearing that her building was slated for a major plumbing job, she interviewed a representative from the firm that had been hired and then published a description of services they would offer residents on individual kitchen and bathroom renovations. In another issue she covered the visit of two residents to the local police precinct to discuss deteriorating conditions that were making that part of town unsightly and unsafe. The paper reported the discussion between the two sides and asked for additional points that could be raised at the next meeting at the station house.

As you see, some editors keep their bulletins light; others prefer to report the nitty-gritty of tenant life. You will find the style of your paper will be determined by 1) what your fellow tenants want to read; 2) the living conditions in your building and in the immediate neighborhood—where much reform is needed you can expect to find yourself a "crusading editor"; 3) how much control you have over the publication. If the building owner is paying print costs and allowing the tenants editorial control (unlikely, but possible), you can be certain he will not tolerate a litany of complaints about how his property is run.

Sponsorship

Who pays for the newsletter may depend on where you live, too. Co-op City, which is located in the Bronx, New York, and is the largest cooperative community in the world, produces a hefty thirty-page tabloid that is distributed every week, without charge, to the 15,000 families living in that mammoth complex. Its sponsor, the United Housing Foundation, picks up the tab although the paper carries a great deal of advertising which obviously pays for most of, if not all, the expenses.

Similarly, multi-family projects administered by a city Housing Authority usually have house organs that are distributed free to tenants.

If an apartment house is large enough or prestigious enough, or if the developer has nationwide interests, it is possible that the owners would underwrite the cost of printing the paper. It is good—and inexpensive—public relations for them. The Heritage Development Group, Inc., developers of Heritage Village, an exclusive adult condominium community in what its owners describe as "Connecticut's rolling countryside," prints a slick fifteen-page newsletter on activities in that Southbury complex. Copies of the paper are free to residents and are included in the company's promotion mailings to prospective Heritage Villagers and others interested in events there. Thus, newsletters are also used for advertising purposes.

You should realize though that if this happens the tenants usually lose control over the newsletter's contents. An editor will be appointed by management and will be on their payroll. He or she may not even live in the building. If tenant life is reasonably serene where you are and your interest is in a sociable bulletin, this would be a perfect situation—a paper without any of the work! But if you all have a few axes to grind, better pay for and print the paper yourselves and leave management out of it.

To be fair, some management-sponsored newsletters do allow an above-the-ground print forum of sorts for tenant opinion. Mr.

Becker, for instance, publishes reports in his newsletters from tenants' representative committees and they contain many of the usual tenant complaints about roaches, disruptive parties, illegal use of the laundry room, and so forth. But if those tenants were irate enough about one management failing or another to institute a rent strike, say, their access to the newsletter would no doubt be cut off immediately.

In a cooperative or a condominium funds for a paper can be appropriated by the board of managers. They will be for production costs only. Rarely will those boards approve even a small salary for a resident-editor.

If outside funding appears impossible in your particular situation, the tenants will have to foot the bill themselves. But it won't be steep, as you will see next.

Production costs

After working out preliminary financing details, visit a print shop for price quotations and some ideas on design. You will see that the most inexpensive newsletter style—and the one used most frequently—is plain bond paper of ordinary twenty-pound weight. The copy is typewritten and then delivered to the printer for duplicating. (Setting type by hand and using paper of a very heavy or glossy stock, although attractive in appearance, is prohibitively expensive.)

Rates for a simple bulletin of that description will vary, of course, but here is what two buildings pay:

The "Homestead Manor Newsletter" in Texas costs $8.50 per 100 copies. It is one legal-size sheet typewritten on both sides of the paper.

In New York, the "250 House Letter" is printed on standard-size white bond with copy on just one side of the paper. A four-page letter of that style—picked up from the printer unstapled—costs $30 for 200 copies of each page. That averages out to $1.80 a year per tenant (the paper is issued monthly).

The newsletter's title, or logo, can also be designed by the printer and will cost about $30. This is a one-time charge, of course.

Photographs are costly to reproduce—about $8.00 apiece—so unless funds are unlimited better forget about them. One editor found a particularly clever and inexpensive way to break up type: black and white artwork and unusual borders clipped from the *New Yorker* magazine (you do not need permission to lift that type of material). Another editor added a dollop of color to her news sheet by using seals, of the type used by schoolchildren, varied according to the season. For example, she stuck on each sheet a flower for the spring, leaves for the fall, and stars at Christmas. For even more variety, you can print the newsletter on a different color paper each month.

Distribution

The paper can be slid under each apartment door or tucked into each mailbox or, if your building has a desk in the lobby, stacked on the counter so that tenants can help themselves to a copy.

It is also a good idea to have a small outside mailing list. Send a copy to the owner of the building and to the real estate reporter and city editor of your local newspaper as well as to your local city and state representatives. Exposure of your newsletter to the media and to legislators is particularly important if your building is waging any kind of war—a rent strike, preservation fight, or co-op or condominium conversion protest. It could mean free publicity for your cause from the newspaper and assistance from the political leaders, who will delight at all those captive voters under one roof. Follow up the mailing of an especially important issue with a telephone call to the addressees telling them the paper is on its way and why you think they would be interested in seeing it. If that issue is announcing the formation of a rent strike protest or a tenants' meeting to fight plans to convert the building to a condominium, or anything else that would be of area interest, send a copy to your local radio and television stations for possible additional coverage.

In buildings with a special camaraderie, tenants who move often ask to have the newsletter sent to them at their new addresses. Whether or not these subscriptions are filled without charge depends on your finances.

Advertising

Editors with a Horatio Alger streak may want to solicit advertisements for the newsletter and turn it into a profit-making part-time job. But this will work only in a *very* large apartment project where a local merchant is sure he is reaching a considerable number of people for his advertising dollar.

Block association newsletters

The mechanics of producing block papers are the same as those for apartment houses. Financing is no problem since the money comes from membership fees paid to the association. Newsletters of this type are issued sporadically, sometimes to report only one specific development, sometimes bi-monthly or quarterly. What goes into them? No personal notes about individual block residents (unless one of them is elected mayor!) or buildings. Since the only purpose of these papers is the dissemination of association news, the content is confined to reports of block meetings, plans for upcoming carnivals or tree plantings or any other civic or social undertaking of the group. One association printed in one of its issues a directory of forty important telephone numbers—local hospitals, poison control center, police, fire, rent office, Board of Health, etc. An excellent idea.

So there it is. Most assuredly publishing a newsletter is work, and it will, like any other job, have a few not-so-charming moments. Is it worth it? A spot check of tenants immediately after publication of the first issue should provide the answer. And if *they're* pleased with the paper—which they will be, unanimously—imagine the pride and delight of its editor!

CHAPTER 11

□

Tipping the Service Staff

It is possible to tell the approach of the Christmas season just by watching the ingratiating smiles and sometimes overall obsequiousness of an apartment house service staff. Yes, even the super. With visions of sugar plums dancing in their heads, building employees are a pleasure to do business with from about December 1 to the end of the year. But lurking behind those dazzling smiles is a calculated "How much will I get?," while the hapless recipients of all that cheer are nervously wondering "How much should I give?" A seasonal trauma peculiar to the apartment dweller, it is time for that annual outflow of cash known as the "Christmas gratuity."

Tipping the management staff can be an unsettling, guilt-ridden, status-laden affair—and costly. In some cases it's downright frightening. One family living in a super-luxury building reports sixty-two employees who expect tips at Christmas. In 1971 they gave to only eighteen of them and considered themselves "skimping, not giving as much as we should." Their gifts that year, in varying amounts to each employee, amounted to $380. In 1972 they cut back, giving $5 where they once handed out $10 and doing away altogether with a handful of $5 envelopes for emergency distribution to anyone who looked untipped. They spent $220 that year. "I think we've leveled off," says the wife. "We're getting older or smarter or poorer. The people who are nice to you are going to be nice whatever you tip."

In a field where weekly salaries may average $100, building employees understandably look forward to their Christmas bonus. And, although the procedure is nerve-wracking and annoying to most tenants, some do enjoy handing out the gift envelopes. "I'm a tipper," says a resident of a lower-middle-class neighborhood who passes out $70 to three employees at Christmas. "I enjoy tipping," echoes another, more affluent apartment dweller. "These porters are making $60 or whatever and you need a hell of a lot more than that to live." In addition to tipping occasionally during the year, at Christmas this tenant gives his custodian $10, the doormen $7.50, and another $7.50 to each of the elevator operators, even though he lives on the ground floor. The super, against whom he has a variety of grievances, gets nothing.

When to tip

In some areas of the country, particularly in the South and the West, holiday tipping is unknown, except at the most luxurious addresses. "When somebody does something nice for me I give him a buck or two at the time," says a Florida tenant, and that is often the way it goes. Or the thank you may be the ubiquitous bottle of Scotch. But at Christmas, nothing. Likewise, tenants living in private homes that have been converted into apartments usually need not grapple with the tipping mystique since they take out their own garbage, make their own repairs, and so forth. Student apartment dwellers are not big tippers (if they bother at all), although young people in general, service personnel have found, are more generous than their older neighbors (many of whom still tip what they did in 1947).

But in large cities anywhere and in buildings where there is a service staff, it is a rare tenant who will risk incurring an employee's scorn by neglecting a Christmas gratuity, regardless of how he may feel about services in the building during the year. Some people do not tip, of course. Estimates of their number vary, but one big-city managing agent says only about one-half of the people in his buildings do not tip. However, a doorman in the same city says he receives gifts from 80 percent of the people under his roof.

So, as we tip a cranky cab driver, a slow waiter, and an all-thumbs hairdresser, we show our appreciation for slapdash or nonexistent apartment house services. As one disgruntled tenant put it: "It's all as intimidating as hell."

Most tenants can cope with giving a handyman a dollar or two for making repairs and the doorman his 25¢ for calling a cab. It is the enormity· of what is expected from them at Christmas by all those smiling faces suddenly appearing from out of the basement that is chilling. So this chapter will concentrate on Yuletide tipping.

The pool gift

To detach themselves from the whole uncomfortable business, an increasing number of tenants are preferring to pool their contributions for a lump-sum presentation to employees. Pool tipping, as it is called, is easier on the psyche and can be less costly than individual gifts. The system can be set up in several different ways: At Manhattan's United Nations Plaza, co-op owners each contribute $140 to a general fund from which payments are made to about thirty employees in each of the two towers. In a medium-sized rental building in Washington, D.C., two volunteers collect whatever their fellow tenants care to toss into a cigar box. The money is then distributed to employees according to length of service. (Their names and dates of employment are obtained from management.) At another high-rise structure, cooperators are asked to contribute one-tenth of their maintenance cost to a "Christmas Fund" set up by the directors. The Christmas-Chanukah fund at still another large complex calls for a donation by residents of a dollar a room for gifts to maintenance workers, security guards, office staff, and gardeners. In most cases the holiday collections are administered by residents; in only a few instances by management.

Pool tipping does have its bad features. Those who are tightfisted get a free ride from the generous. And since the gifts are often presented as coming from "the tenants," workers do not always know who belongs to which group. Although building-service employees unions take no official stand on pooling, the system is unpopular with almost all service personnel for the obvious reason that individual gifts usually amount to more than a shared general fund would provide. Funds also are subject to deductions for income taxes and Social Security. Incidentally, your cash gifts to the building staff may be tax deductible. If you work at home the gifts may be considered a business expense. The limit is $25 per person and you will have to keep records of the payments. It is best to check your local tax office however, since it's one of those very small print clauses that need professional interpretation.

Back to pool tipping. If you plan to inaugurate the pool gift in your building next Christmas, you might expect some volatile opposition. That is what happened at a 1,000-unit rental building in one big city. Its residents were attending a special meeting to decide on a new tipping system for lobby personnel that year. At one point the president of the group interrupted the lively exchange to announce that the men went to management and threatened to go on strike en masse if there were not individual tips. The leader went on to tell those assembled that the threat was no surprise since some of the ranking staff, such as doormen, now made as much as $3,000 each year in tips over Christmas. Together, the twelve employees pulled in about $30,000 in tips each year.

The pool plan at that building was eventually abandoned, although the tenants used the system for tipping such behind-the-scenes employees as basement workers and porters. A good idea for these people since they are often forgotten and a group gift is almost always more than they would take in from individual tenant tips. Actually, if your building or complex is large enough to require the services of full-time gardeners, security people, switchboard operators, and so forth, a pool setup may be essential to keep you all from celebrating Christmas in the poor house.

Individual tipping

If it is not possible to initiate a pool system, you can still get through the holidays, tipping-wise, without making mistakes that will have you sneaking out service entrances for the next year in order to avoid the staff out front.

The first thing to bear in mind is that you cannot ask anyone for advice. Your friends and neighbors will have their own budgets to stay within and obligations to the maintenance crew that are different from yours. The doorman who does no more than say a pleasant good morning to you all year, for instance, may have arranged to keep an eye on your next-door neighbors' children every day while they wait for the school bus. Naturally their gift envelope will contain a few extra Christmas greens.

Building managing agents are reluctant to give advice on individual donations, although they will on occasion handle the distribution of pool gifts. "We've always felt tipping was something that should be left to the conscience of the individual tenant, depending on the service he has gotten during the year," says the president of one firm.

A few realty offices, although they do not take the initiative in guiding tenants through the tipping maze, will make suggestions if approached. Charles Greenthal, president of Charles Greenthal, Inc., a large Manhattan agency, makes the following recommendations for tenants in that region: $6 to a doorman, $9 to a handyman, and $15 to a superintendent.

Asking the employees themselves for direction is out of the question. For one thing, only Form 1040 knows for sure what their annual haul is—they are that close-mouthed. Anyway, you would probably be quoted an inflated figure of what your neighbors are giving. With a genius born of necessity, an employee's psychological attack, guaranteed to reap a rich harvest, goes like this: To one group of tenants (and he *knows* which ones deserve this ploy) a doorman will lament about how many people forgot him and how terrible he feels to find his year's work gone unappreciated. This heart-wringing tale will make the questioner feel that at least he or she will do right by the poor soul. The result is a tip larger than originally anticipated. To the other type the doorman will, with remarkable instinct, impart the information that he is so lucky to be in a building where the residents appreciate him, especially at Christmas and with surprising generosity, too. This brings out the competitive spirit and the desire to out-tip the Joneses. Don't ask the staff.

The amounts listed below will guide you along the lines of what is generally considered adequate tipping. The key word is "generally." Naturally, gifts will vary from one type of building to another and in different sections of the country. Think about your relationship with the service staff in your building or complex. Honestly. And then let your conscience be your guide.

THE SUPERINTENDENT (OR JANITOR): $10 TO $25   Traditionally, he gets the biggest allotment. If you are determined to cut corners this year, don't begin here, even if his service has left almost everything to be desired. He *is* the most important employee in your building (and knows it!) and falling into disfavor with him could mean waiting seventeen days to have your air conditioner fixed during a heat wave next July. Blackmail, surely, but worth it.

If your building has a deskman, he ranks just below the superintendent in the apportionment of Christmas spoils.

Resident managers are a shady area. In many buildings the only contact they have with tenants is taking their rent checks once a month. If your manager seems removed from tenant activity to the point where you would feel embarrassed tipping him, don't. If, on the other hand, he is on the premises full-time and has done special favors for you during the year, Christmas is the time to show your appreciation. Talk to some of your fellow tenants to see whether they offer gratuities to this employee.

THE DOORMAN: $5 TO $10 If you are single and the doorman called a cab for you a couple of rainy mornings during the past year, $5 may be sufficient. If you are a couple and the doorman has gotten a cab for you occasionally and perhaps carried in a few packages, $10 is fine. A family with children might feel they have to give more. A doorman is one service employee you are probably tipping now and then during the year, too, so that might affect the size of your Christmas gift.

ELEVATOR OPERATORS: $5 TO $10 Here again it is a question of how much contact you have with the person you are tipping. One mother of three teenage daughters gives the night elevator crew in her building more because they keep an eye on the girls when they come in late and see them safely upstairs. If for one reason or another you feel more indebted to the day staff, tip accordingly.

THE HANDYMEN: $3 TO $5 They too are sometimes tipped at the time they complete a specific job. Note that supers and handymen should be tipped only for a job beyond the call of duty. That is to say they are not tipped for repairing the bathroom sink, but are if they help install your shelf system.

Tipping during the year will not, unfortunately, carry you through the holidays empty-handed. In the flurry of collecting gift envelopes, employees will forget your generosity over the last eleven months, and you will stand out as merely another Yuletide deadbeat. Spread out your tips during the year if you must conserve, so that you do not have to skip Christmas.

One final point. Bringing back a token gift for the super who took in your mail the week you were on vacation is an excellent idea. But at Christmas do give money, not home-baked goodies, liquor, or ties. Hard cold cash is what all building employees expect in an otherwise warmhearted season.

Moving outside the apartment building, there are others with outstretched palms to consider.

A gift of $3 to $5 should be sufficient for delivery boys (newspapers, supermarket and so forth) and for mailmen, milkmen and laundrymen. You may feel garage attendants should receive that amount or possibly more. A once-a-week cleaning woman could be given a gift. Often she is tipped one day's wages. That may seem a little high, but good cleaning women are hard to come by so one tends to be lavish towards a jewel.

Many, many people, especially in these tight-money days, do not tip any neighborhood service people at Christmas. If you are a new tenant or if you haven't been tipping but think you should be, it is best to ask your neighbors what the practice is in your building or complex. While tips to the super and doorman are an institution, gratuities to some outside people may not be. However, if it is not customary to tip the mailman, say, that does not mean you should ignore him at Christmas if he has been especially kind and helpful during the year. One elderly disabled woman says her mailman takes outgoing mail from her at the time he makes his morning rounds, to save her a trip to the mailbox. Naturally she remembers him when the holidays roll around.

Some women feel they should tip their hairdressers at Christmas even though they have been tipped regularly during the year. Either money or a present is suitable here. Not exactly in the area of gratuities, but on the question of what to give those outside of one's family and friends, a child's teacher should be given a present, never money.

That should take care of everybody. And do remember, the Lord loves a cheerful giver.

CHAPTER 12

□

Where to Complain

If the plumbing is broken or the elevators aren't working, or there is some other serious problem in your apartment or in the building, call the superintendent or resident manager and he or she will arrange to have it fixed promptly.

At least that's the way it's *supposed* to work. But sometimes weeks or even months go by and no workmen show up. Meanwhile, it's nearing summer and your air-conditioner is still broken. Or plaster is raining down from the living room ceiling and what was that about paint chips and lead poisoning?

Maybe your complaint is in another area. You moved out two months ago, and the landlord still hasn't refunded your security deposit.

If you have gotten no satisfaction from on-premises personnel, write a letter. Always make complaints or requests to your landlord in writing. Grim as it sounds you never know when a simple problem will escalate into a lawsuit. Oral promises can count in court, but what can be seen in print looks more professional and is certainly more durable. If your letters to management have brought either empty promises or no response at all, you will have to decide how you want to proceed next. If your problem involves other tenants as well as yourself, it may be more effective if you all band together in seeking some resolution (See Chapter 9, "Tenant Organizing"). But assuming the problem is yours alone, you can proceed in several ways:

First you can write off the security deposit. In the area of repairs, you can forget about them, too, or you can make them yourself and pay the cost out of your own pocket.

Second, you can make the repairs yourself and deduct the amount from next month's rent. This is tricky though. Better check with your local housing or rent office to see what the laws are in your area. In California, for instance, there is a laundry list of qualifications to the statute and set procedures for tenants to follow in order to deduct such expenses.

Third, you can withhold rent until the repairs are made. Another perilous tactic. Be sure to contact your local tenant organization or a lawyer before you attempt it. Rent withholding *is* grounds for eviction. Although in some areas it can be done with the sanction of the court, it is usually permitted only if conditions in your apartment make the place uninhabitable; that is, there is no heat or hot water or perhaps no electricity (*not* that the landlord refuses to fix the air conditioner, or a similar small repair job that the courts may indeed not even consider the landlord's responsibility).

Fourth, you can appeal to local authorities, who will keep after the landlord until the unsafe conditions are corrected. The following is a list of those agencies, although their exact names and specific responsibilities may vary somewhat from one community to another. We will begin with city agencies.

City agencies

HEALTH DEPARTMENT Call here if there are rats or cockroaches in the apartment or building. The owner may be required to provide extermination free to tenants. This office also handles complaints about lack of hot water, inadequate heat, out-of-order plumbing, insufficient garbage cans, rubbish on the premises, and any other unsanitary living conditions.

FIRE DEPARTMENT   Complaints about unsafe gas heaters and appliances, an inadequate fire escape system and lack of fire extinguishers in the building can be registered here.

HUMAN RIGHTS COMMISSION   If you've been discriminated against in housing because of your race, creed or national origin, report it to this office. They enforce the human rights law. There may be a similar bureau operating on the state level. Very few states have laws forbidding sex discrimination, however. The National Organization for Women would like to see a copy of women tenants' letters of complaint to local agencies charging discrimination. NOW's address: 47 East 19th Street, New York, N.Y. 10003. Or write your local NOW chapter.

BUILDING INSPECTION DEPARTMENT/BUILDINGS DEPART-MENT   Most cities have housing codes which place specific responsibilities on the landlord. These are minimum standards to ensure the safety and health of the tenants. If the building owner allows conditions to fall below these standards, he can be taken to court. This city agency (not to be confused with the Housing Authority, which supervises public housing projects) acts princi-pally on maintaining those standards. Register complaints with them on structural or electrical defects; overcrowding; inadequate lighting in hallways; peeling paint and plaster; leaking roofs; lack of plumbing facilities; out-of-service elevators; broken windows; lack of security; lack of sufficient janitorial services.

Bear in mind that in reporting housing code violations you may win the battle but lose the war. The city may close your building. Also, if the landlord owns a number of marginally slum dwellings, he usually knows very well how to skirt code violations. Maybe he will make a few minor repairs to keep the department off his back, and then coast. Or he may be paying off inspectors. This is one agency where corruption often flourishes.

Finally, few leases hold that a landlord *must* take care of violations, so technically he is not violating your agreement.

RENT OFFICE   An arm of the Housing Department in major urban areas, this bureau will answer questions about lease provisions, rent exemptions, or rent control.

CONSUMER AFFAIRS DEPARTMENT   Register with this office any bad dealings you have had with brokers or managing agents, or with any real-estate-related businesses, such as roommate placement services and apartment finding agencies. In many areas of the country the law enforcement powers of this office are slight, if they exist at all, but the Consumer Affairs Department *can* effectively lobby for stricter legislation in problem areas, and they do manage to get good media attention for the shady businesses they flush out. Here again there may be a similar bureau operating on the state level.

Every state now has at least one nongovernmental consumer group. Do register your grievances with them and offer any assistance you can to help these organizations get legislation enacted to protect tenants' rights. The Oregon Consumer League, for instance, worked for several years on a package of laws that ranged from security deposit refunds to a landlord's right of accessibility to apartments without a tenant's permission. They recently had the satisfaction of seeing more than three-quarters of their proposals signed into law. But first they had to be told by individual tenants and building councils just what the problem areas were.

HOUSING COURT   Operating in only a few areas around the country, Housing Courts have been set up as part of Civil Courts to settle landlord–tenant disputes. Tenants do not need a lawyer but, as with small claims courts, larger landlords are frequently represented by counsel. The courts hear principally housing code violations, non-payment of rent and demolition and receivership cases. But judges and/or hearing officers dip into other areas as well. Boston's Housing Court recently ruled that a tenant group had the right to pin anti-landlord bulletins on management's property. Some tenants criticize the courts as being subtly, or even blatantly, pro-landlord; many more are satisfied with verdicts.

It should be noted here that cooperative and condominium owners are in no special situation in filing complaints about unsafe or unhealthy conditions in their buildings. If the board of managers will not allocate funds to repair housing code violations, the appropriate city agency can penalize the corporation or homeowners' association the way it would any building owner. Aren't you, in effect, penalizing yourself? Yes, but if a sluggish board will not allocate funds—funds which may already be in hand—to make vital repairs, a nudge from a city agency may be needed to get them going, in the same way that landlords of rental buildings may sometimes have to be prodded.

State agencies

OFFICE OF THE SECRETARY OF STATE, DIVISION OF LICENSES   Handles licenses for and complaints against a variety of business people operating in the state, including real estate brokers and salespersons.

ATTORNEY GENERAL'S OFFICE OR DEPARTMENT OF REAL ESTATE   Deals with irregular practices in land sales and, in states with well-formulated laws, complaints about cooperative or condominium conversions and new cooperative or condominium offering plans.

Can the landlord "get you" if you bring the health department or some other governmental agency down on him? He could try.

You might get a notice that your rent is being increased, which is one way of getting back at you. Or management could try to evict you. This is called a "retaliatory eviction." He will simply give you a thirty-day notice terminating your tenancy in his building and give no reason for doing so. If you have a lease you are pretty safe, but if you are a holdover tenant, you may have to go to court. Retaliatory evictions for reporting housing code violations are increasingly being ruled illegal, however, so if you can prove that the landlord is forcing you out because you reported him, you will win the suit. But you must be a model tenant otherwise so that the eviction could have been prompted only by that one incident.

Outside agencies

If the aforementioned authorities cannot help you, you can take your case to outside agencies. Or you can hire a lawyer and sue your landlord in a full-fledged court case. But first let's look at the outside agencies.

    Tenant councils   Perhaps you need go no further than your building or neighborhood tenant council. A Philadelphia woman with no previous knowledge that one existed wandered into a tenant headquarters building in her neighborhood and found that they represented her apartment house. They took her case to their arbitration panel, and it was settled to her satisfaction—and at no cost to her. Many tenant groups retain legal counsel, or are partially staffed by volunteer lawyers, who are willing and even delighted to fight for tenant cases, especially ones they consider particularly interesting or of "landmark" status.

    In any event, the very least you can expect from a tenant council is some guidance on how to proceed with your problem and an up-to-date report on what legislation, if any, has been passed in your area of concern. If you're trying to get your security deposit back, for example, it would be helpful to know if your state has passed a law requiring landlords to pay interest to tenants on security monies. That bit of knowledge could affect the size of the check you are trying to get back.

SMALL CLAIMS COURT   Small Claims Courts are designed to make it easier for the "little people" to bring suit without the expense of hiring a lawyer.

Although most claims are filed by consumers charging businesses with poor service or defective merchandise or by businesses seeking collection of debts, landlords and tenants can have their day in court too. In fact, a 1971 Consumer Union survey found that landlord-tenant suits accounted for 30 percent of all small claims cases brought by consumers. Most of these suits concern the ubiquitous security deposit refunds, but tenants also have other grievances against the landlord—a faultily installed shelf that toppled and broke an expensive set of dishes, or a neglected bathroom leak that ultimately drowned an expensive wall-to-wall carpet. A tenant may also want to sue a subletter who agreed to rent an apartment for six months and then took off for parts unknown after three. Landlords hauling tenants into court are usually seeking back rent or damages to their property. No evictions, though; they're handled in another, lower state court.

Small Claims Courts are enjoying a renaissance these days, but for a while they were considered merely vast collection agencies for retail stores, finance companies, landlords, and other businesses. Ralph Nader's 1972 Study Group on the subject found that "for the vast majority of American consumers Small Claims Courts are either unavailable, unusable or invisible."

Some of those points are all too true. With his fingers walking over half the telephone book, the consumer has a hard time even *finding* the court in many areas. In New York and a few other cities the courts now have evening and Saturday sessions, but in the vast majority of states, bringing suit requires missing work to attend a weekday court session. And wages lost cannot be added to a claim. The wave of consumerism that began in the late 1960s is changing many of those gripes, however, and the growing number of consumers approaching the court are beginning to balance the scales that had been lopsided with complaints by merchants.

The greatest attraction of suing in Small Claims Court is the relative ease of the procedure. After you have decided to bring suit against, say, the owner of your building, first track down his (or his company's) correct name. This is very important. In some cases the suit may be dismissed unless you have identified the company exactly as it has registered itself for legal purposes, right down to the "Inc." And make sure you have the name of the *owner* of the building—not the superintendent or the managing or rental agent. This may turn out to be quite a revelation. Many tenants have no idea who actually owns the roof over their heads, having dealt only with individuals or organizations retained by the owner. Your Buildings Department or tax assessor's office can tell you who your landlord is.

You can sue only for money. You cannot bring suit for return of property, negligence, slander, poor service, lack of repairs, harassment or trespassing, unless a money value can be put on those charges. So for this type of conflict another means of settlement will have to be found. Small Claims Courts have a reimbursement ceiling that hovers around $500; if your damages are substantially higher you will either have to write off the difference or take the case to a regular court.

Small Claims Courts are listed in the telephone book under city, county or state government. In some areas of the country they have other names—justice of the peace courts, conciliation courts, magistrate's courts, sometimes a mixture of all of them. In New Orleans, for example, it's city court; elsewhere in Louisiana small claims suits are handled by justice of the peace courts.

States with especially well-structured court systems—California, Wisconsin, Massachusetts, Connecticut, Washington, New York, and New Jersey—offer residents free "How to Sue" booklets that list addresses of the courts, maps showing how to get there and other information needed to file suit and conduct oneself in court. If your area isn't mentioned above, contact your state Attorney General's Office anyway. Several states have pamphlets in the works that should be off the presses soon.

Once you've got an address, call the clerk of the court to see how you file suit and where you report. You will have to appear in person to file and will be charged a court fee of $3 to $15. If you win the judgment, the fee is refunded. After you fill out the form giving particulars on whom you are suing, the clerk will assign you a date, place, and time to appear for a hearing. It usually takes about a month to come to trial, although the wait can sometimes be only ten days to two weeks. This wait is still faster than a regular court case where crowded calendars usually mean a wait of months, even a year.

Once your suit has been filed, a summons to appear in court will go out to the other party either by registered mail or issued by a sheriff, constable, bailiff or some private citizen. When your opponent sees the summons and knows that you mean business (the repeated phone calls and registered letters meant nothing), he may offer to settle out of court—in fact that is how 80–90 percent of all cases are resolved. If he does this and you agree to what he is offering, have him put the terms of the settlement in writing, both of you sign the paper and leave it to be filed with the court so that the agreement can be enforced. Include reimbursement of the court costs you have already paid since they would probably have been awarded you had you won the judgment.

If the other party makes a decent offer, you would do well to consider accepting it. You'll save the time and expense (especially if you stand to lose a day's pay) of a court case. And if it comes out in court that you rejected an out-of-court settlement, the judge may subconsciously label you a crank, no doubt prejudicing your case.

On the day of the trial, bring all your papers pertaining to the case along with you—bills, receipts, correspondence with the defendant. The correspondence can mean a good deal since it shows that you tried to settle your dispute amicably outside court. The tenant with the broken dishes should sweep them into a cardboard box and bring the box with him; the one with the bathroom leak brings the ruined carpet, or at least a sizable section of it.

In New York, the District of Columbia, Iowa, Kansas, Minnesota, Ohio, West Virginia, Wisconsin and Wyoming, you will be allowed the choice of a judge or an arbitrator to hear your case. Both you and the defendant must agree which. The bad feature of the arbitrator is that his decision cannot be appealed, although appealing a judge's decision is expensive and seldom successful. Another point that might work against you is that the arbitrator is usually a lawyer and if the defendant is a lawyer representing your landlord, the arbitrator may unconsciously side with a brother lawyer, whereas a judge would be more likely— again unconsciously—to side with the underdog on the legal knowledge scale: you. Studies made in New York City have also found arbitrators more likely to make compromise decisions than judges would. You will get something, that is, but probably not as much as you wanted. Take the judge.

What if the defendant does not show up in court? In all likelihood after the judge or arbitrator looks over your claim, you will win by default.

When both parties are present, a decision is usually reached the same day as the trial. If the judge or arbitrator needs more time, a postcard will be sent to both parties within a few days announcing who won and the amount of the judgment, if any.

So you win. Now how do you collect? The 1971 *Consumer Reports* survey on small claims courts found that in one out of five cases you will not be able to collect the money you've won, even though it was awarded to you by law. How come? In some instances the defendant has filed bankruptcy, or his business may have folded since you won the case. This is more likely to happen if you've sued the Slim-Eze Reducing Spa than a landlord who will be in town for a long while, but if by some chance he is a developer who *does* go bankrupt, hold on to that court decision. A judgment is collectable for ten or twenty years, so if he is back on the board within that time you can probably collect your money. The same goes for the slippery sublet who stuck you with nine months' rent. When he surfaces again, slap him with collection papers.

The collection process for small claims differs from state to state, but most likely the problem will be put in the hands of the sheriff, marshal or constable who will seek to collect your money for you. Fees for the process will be charged to the defendant, although in some areas that $10 or so charge is non-refundable. Yes, that is unfair.

If *you're* being sued, read the complaint closely. If it is accurate, pay up and save yourself the time spent in court where the verdict would be against you anyway. If you think it is unjust, collect your material and arrange for witnesses. If you need more time, try to have the trial date moved back.

Don't let having to appear in court intimidate you. One woman shied away from filing a just claim because she was "too embarrassed to talk in front of all those people." What people? The procedure at Small Claims Court is far simpler and less held to strict rules than a regular court is. There is no jury, and lawyers are not necessary. In some states they are even barred from appearing. This does not apply in some cases where one side is a large corporation. There an attorney for the company is permitted to appear as the defendant. But even this shouldn't bother you. The judge will know you have no legal expertise and will bend over backwards to see that the talk doesn't bubble over with whereases and witness thereofs. Lawyers, in fact, have complained that, overall, Small Claims Courts are weighted in favor of the consumer.

BETTER BUSINESS BUREAU   You know you can turn to the Better Business Bureau to report misleading advertising or to lodge a complaint against an unscrupulous merchant. But can the bureaus intercede in landlord–tenant disputes?

Some can and others won't. In New York City, landlord–tenant headache capital of the world, callers with housing problems are referred immediately by the BBB to appropriate city agencies. But in other cities—Philadelphia, Denver and San Francisco are good examples—the BBB pitches in to do what it can for beleaguered tenants. Unfortunately, they can't always do much, as you will see later.

The more than 130 Better Business Bureaus operating in the United States were organized for the protection of the consumer long before the cause became fashionable. The bureaus are funded by membership dues collected from companies doing business locally. Dues are determined either by a company's size or its gross sales. However, complaints can be filed against any firm, not just those who support the BBB. There is no charge, of course, to anyone calling for information or seeking to register a grievance.

With the growing interest in consumerism over the last ten years, and the emergence of newer, more militant consumer groups, the BBB appeared for a time to be left behind in the dust. But now they're sprucing up their image and are back in the ring. The upgrading dates back to 1970 when the Council of Better Business Bureaus was organized to standardize procedures nationally and to make the service more effective. The council has management headquarters in New York City and operations headquarters in Washington, D.C.

One of the major complaints against the bureaus has been that since they are sponsored by the business community, they are soft on patrolling member firms and indeed those merchants receive preferential treatment in complaint cases. Not so, says the BBB. Of course there are member companies with poor business practices, but the overwhelming majority of those supporting the BBB are, in fact, doing so to drive the bad guys out. The bureaus are also criticized because they do not represent every business in town. That is true enough, since membership in several large urban centers averages less than 10 percent of all firms operating in the area.

Despite its alleged faults, however, the BBB does draw beleaguered consumers. Total number of complaints or inquiries to all BBBs average about 8 million a year. The overwhelming majority of complaint cases are settled in favor of the complainant, perhaps not to his complete satisfaction, but the BBB considers a favorable settlement one in which the consumer comes out ahead—no matter how slight the adjustment.

Here is how it works in the field of real estate. Say you are interested in checking on the reputation of a land development company in the southwest where you'd like to purchase one of God's little acres. You can (indeed you *should*) call the nearest BBB for a report on the outfit, even though it is operating out of a distant state. The BBB keeps a master list of national companies that is compiled in the headquarters office in Washington and then circulated to all regional bureaus. Local offices, of course, also keep their own files on area businesses.

When you call for information, an operator will give you one of four standard replies to your query: an "A" rating on the company means that files on the business show no customer complaints; a "B" stands for a satisfactory performance by the company and any complaints that have been received were settled satisfactorily; a rating of "C" means that the company does not meet BBB standards at that time. The operator will then go on to tell why this is so in one of five standard explanations: 1) they have a record of unanswered complaints; 2) they have a record of failing to settle complaints; 3) they have failed to eliminate the cause of complaints; 4) they use questionable selling practices or 5) misleading or inaccurate statements in advertising. If there is a "D" on the company card, you will be told the BBB has no information on the firm.

Complaints against a service or retail establishment must be made in writing. After your letter is received, the BBB will usually send you a form to fill in and return. Actually it's just as well you don't bother calling unless you must. Another complaint against the bureaus is their appalling telephone service. Constant busy signals or phones that ring and ring and ring are more likely to be found in urban areas where the bureaus have too few personnel and too many callers, but regardless of the reasons for it, it is irritating.

As stated earlier, whether your local BBB can help in landlord–tenant problems depends entirely on its willingness to step into that sensitive area. Dan Bell, president of the Denver-based Rocky Mountain BBB, says: "We've adopted a philosophy of being an umbrella on all consumer problems, regardless of their nature. A good percentage of the total volume of complaints received here are against landlords." Most of these, Mr. Bell goes on to say, are for landlords' refusal to refund security deposits. These situations, he adds, usually end in a compromise between the two sides. Other tenant gripes are about rent hikes and landlord harassment, but these the bureau cannot handle and complainants are referred to local regulatory agencies. (This is the pattern for other regional BBBs that handle tenant problems. They, too, are overwhelmingly asked to mediate in security deposit disputes.)

Aside from security deposits, but still of specific tenant interest, BBBs will handle grievances against apartment locating services, a new development on the rental scene that is giving headaches to many state regulating agencies, and against roommate placement services, another relatively new enterprise, but one that is much better run.

It is important to remember, however, that the Better Business Bureau is merely a conscience; it has no law-enforcing powers. All it can do is send a letter to the merchant against whom a complaint has been lodged, asking him what he intends to do about giving the customer satisfaction. But if a commercial establishment—or a landlord—has consistently poor business practices, it is not likely they will be moved by an appeal to their supposedly better natures. Press releases that the BBB sends to local newspapers mentioning names of concerns against whom a battery of complaints have been filed are a stronger nudge for them to straighten up and fly right. Bear in mind, too, that grievances against a product or service are often solved to the satisfaction of the consumer because businesses depend on satisfied customers for their livelihood and will make adjustments just for that reason. A landlord–tenant situation does not provide that motivation. This is especially true in a locale where apartments are scarce. If a tenant complains, who cares? There'll be another one along in a hurry, so no need to worry about good will. Unless the landlord is a multimillion-dollar corporation, it is unlikely anyone in the community will even know who he is if they did want to attack his professional reputation.

Summing up, here is what the BBB *cannot* do: give legal advice, recommend a product or service, give information about a firm's credit rating, help you out when you've neglected to read the fine print in a lease or contract, salve your wounds when you've bought an air conditioner for $200 that a store down the street is offering for $150—or, depending on where you live, help out with your landlord problems.

Better Business Bureaus are beginning to utilize the arbitration table for consumer complaints. At this writing, however, the service is spotty, operating in only about thirty of the BBB's 130 bureaus, although in the planning stage at another seventy-five.

When a local BBB is unable to resolve a dispute between a customer and a merchant through persuasion, it may suggest that the disputants agree to binding arbitration. Both parties submit signed statements of their positions, and then a date, place and time for a hearing is set. Usually it is an evening or weekend so that no one will miss work. Meetings are held at an area BBB office or some other neutral territory.

In theory, anyone can serve as a BBB arbitrator and the bureaus' pools include attorneys, students, housewives, retirees and educators. They serve without pay and are trained by the BBB.

Besides the arbitrator, consumer, and businessman, an administrator from the area BBB may attend the hearings. No lawyers for either side are required. The meetings are much like those of any other collective bargaining agency. The arbitrator explains the rules and procedures and then each person has a chance to elaborate on his written statement, without interruption. The arbitrator asks appropriate questions, and when he is satisfied that there is nothing more to be added by either side, the meeting is adjourned. The arbitrator's ruling is made in writing from the BBB to both parties within ten to thirty days.

There is no charge to either consumer or businessman, except in Cleveland, Pittsburgh, and Miami, where arbitration hearings are conducted under the auspices of the American Arbitration Association. In these cities both disputing parties must pay a small administrative fee ranging from $5 to $12 for the consumer, slightly more for the merchant.

It is still too early to predict the effect Better Business Bureau arbitration practices will have on landlords and tenants. Since some BBBs are now involved in working out security-deposit disputes, the hearings may be helpful in other areas as well where there is a product or sum of money involved. In weightier housing problems, however, the part-time volunteer arbitrators may be over their heads, if they decide to mediate in such issues at all. In those cases a tenant or tenant group would do better to employ arbitration personnel who are trained to deal in more complex issues.

Other arbitrators

AMERICAN ARBITRATION ASSOCIATION Until recently, practically all tribunal activities of the 35,000-member American Arbitration Association, the only nationwide, non-governmental center for private dispute settlement, fell into one of three categories: labor grievances in private employment, business disputes, and automobile insurance claims.

Those cases still predominate, but social changes have created new areas of conflict in which the AAA is being asked to mediate: students and school administrators over institution rules; racial and ethnic groups in urban areas over the dispersal of public funds for antipoverty programs; consumers and retailers over product quality; and yes, tenants and landlords over the perform- ance of their mutual responsibilities.

The AAA does not merely sit back and wait for quarreling clients. Its Washington, D.C.-based National Center for Dispute Settlement, a separate division of the association, was formed in 1968 to enter into these new conflict areas and to try to develop new systems for conflict resolution. The NCDS has assisted the Department of Housing and Urban Development in the develop- ment of a model lease and grievance procedure, and right now they are working with local housing authorities in the election of Tenant Advisory Councils and grievance hearing affairs.

If you or your tenant group have a housing complaint—lack of repairs promised by the landlord, return of security deposit, eviction threat, rent withholding for management concessions— you may find the arbitration procedure less time-consuming, irritating, and costly than a court case. This is especially true in gray areas where both sides have a point and a few small concessions on the part of the tenant(s) are better than losing outright in court.

How does the process work? First, check your lease. They are still in the minority, but a growing number of leases contain clauses requiring feuding tenants and landlords to submit to binding arbitration. These are usually found in buildings where tenants have conducted rent strikes and won the clause as a concession. In fact, trying to get the landlord to agree to approach the bargaining table is sometimes the *cause* of a strike.

The NCDS will arbitrate in both public and private housing segments and between individual tenants and their landlords, as well as with building councils. The last group, even without an arbitration clause in their lease, naturally have more strength in approaching a landlord than a single tenant would. For him it will be difficult to get the landlord to the mediator, but since the word arbitration has a softer ring than "lawsuit," the lone tenant may be successful. Both sides must agree to the hearing.

Landlords can instigate the process, too. Although they are usually seeking eviction or collection of back rent, their grievances can also run the gamut. One landlord brought a complaint against a tenant whom he accused of breaking and entering the basement of his apartment house. Since the tenant was anxious for someone to hear his side, he readily agreed to arbitration. The arbitrator found that the landlord had failed on several occasions to provide proper heating and water for several tenants in the house, and the "breaking and entering" was the result of the tenants' efforts to restore those vital services. (This is a good example of the "gray areas" mentioned earlier. Entering another's house without permission is punishable by law, but in the arbitration procedure extenuating circumstances can be taken into account.)

Recognizing the landlord's right to protect his property from damage, the arbitrator developed an agreement which would allow certain specified tenants the right to enter the basement on a "need" basis if and when they were accompanied by the landlord. Conflicts leading up to that impasse were also discussed, leading to a reduction of the problems that had existed between the two sides.

The National Center for Dispute Settlement has offices in the following cities:

National Headquarters
1212 Sixteenth St., N.W.
Washington, D.C. 20036
(202) 628-1545

Local Operations
Boston
294 Washington St.
Boston, Mass. 02108

Cleveland
    215 Euclid Ave. #630
    Cleveland, Ohio 44114
Jackson
    Post Office Drawer 290
    Jackson, Miss. 39205
Los Angeles
    2333 Beverly Blvd.
    Los Angeles, Calif. 90057
Philadelphia
    115 Witherspoon Bldg.
    Juniper & Walnut Streets
    Philadelphia, Pa. 19107
Rochester
    36 West Main Street
    Rochester, N.Y. 14614
San Francisco
    One Kearny Street
    San Francisco, Calif. 94108
Seattle
    720 3rd Ave., Suite 909
    Seattle, Wash. 98104

Tenants who do not live near one of these cities can call one of the American Arbitration Association's twenty-two regional offices across the country, where they will be put in touch with NCDS panel members who travel to outlying areas. All that is needed for a hearing is a tenant, his landlord, and the arbitrator. Lawyers for either side are not necessary. Both sides should bring to the meeting any correspondence or receipts pertaining to the case. After each party presents his side of the story, the arbitrator asks a few questions and, usually the same day, makes his legally binding decision. Sometimes the decision follows a few days later.

Although the AAA does little advertising (occasionally they will run a full-page magazine advertisement headed with their slogan "Maybe your day in court shouldn't be in court"), the arbitration process as it applies to landlord–tenant relations is growing. The case load in the San Francisco Bay Area, for example, is so heavy the NCDS office there has now assigned a full-time employee just to mediate housing controversies, most of which come from the activist Berkeley and Oakland areas.

Tenants who have used the process appear satisfied with the arbitrators' decisions, although sometimes the verdicts result in a compromise between the two sides. Arbitrators say confidentially that just the chance to state his grievance to an interested listener without interruption is often a large part of a tenant's satisfaction. Rudy Tolbert, director of the Northwest Tenants Organization, which represents twenty private and public apartment houses in a section of Philadelphia, says his group has been successful in having an arbitration clause written into the leases of eighteen of those buildings. They have had to seek out the NCDS twice and have had no trouble with landlord followthrough of the arbitrator's directives.

There is a charge for arbitration. Although the forty-seven-year-old AAA is supported in part by foundation grants, it still depends on charges to disputants for a sizable portion of its income. The fee is 3 percent of claims up to $10,000, with a minimum charge of $50. The bill is either split between tenant and landlord, or the party filing the complaint pays initially and the arbitrator decides if an adjustment should be made. Even with the charge, arbitration has several points over some of its competitors.

If you succeed in getting the clause in your building's lease, you are almost guaranteed peaceful settlement of management quarrels ever after. No lawyers, court cases, high fees. Unlike the Better Business Bureau, the AAA has law-enforcement powers. Its judgments constitute a court order.

It is faster than Small Claims Court, where there may be a long wait for a trial date that is then set at an inconvenient hour. Arbitration hearings can be set up as soon as twenty-four hours after a regional NCDS office receives a call from tenant or landlord. The meetings can be held at any time of the day, although there is a $5 per hour extra charge for meetings held after 6 P.M. weekdays or on Saturdays, Sundays or legal holidays.

The process is flexible, too, and not held to strict rules of evidence in the way that a court is. Finally, although Small Claims Court will usually not handle suits over $500, there is no ceiling on AAA claims. No minimum either, for that matter.

In fact, there is only one disadvantage to arbitration (aside from the possible difficulty of getting the landlord to the bargaining table in the first place), and that is, as in Small Claims Court, that the arbitrator's decision cannot be appealed. But then appealing a judge's decision is expensive and rarely successful.

There are other arbitrators in addition to the American Arbitration Association and the Better Business Bureau, although they operate on a much smaller scale than these organizations. (Unfortunately, because of space limitations, no mention can be made of the numerous small, regional arbitration groups around the country.)

RABBINICAL COURTS   Many rabbis across the country—of all branches of Judaism—will sit in on landlord–tenant conflicts and will render decisions that are binding by law, as in any arbitration settlement. Some of the clerics operate singly, others are organized into permanent courts. One of the latter is rabbinical court.

Guided by Deuteronomy ("Judges and officers shalt thou make thee in all thy gates, which the Lord thy God giveth thee, tribe by tribe; and they shall judge the people with righteous judgment"), rabbinical courts have traditionally settled personal and family problems such as divorce, conversion, and intermarriage for 3,000 years. They became fewer in number with the dissolution of ghetto life. Today there are only about a half dozen rabbinical courts in the United States, but their special system of justice is far from dying, and their arbitration has extended to tenant–landlord relations. One court deserves special mention:

the Rabbinical Court of Justice of the Associated Synagogues of Massachusetts, which has been especially involved in the tenant scene in Boston. The court's administrator, Rabbi Samuel I. Korff, entered Boston's troubled South End housing area in the late 1960s. This was an urban renewal area that was beginning to regain some of its 19th-century popularity. The black tenants and long-time residents of the area claimed that the renewal involved wanton demolition and unsatisfactory relocation. The Jewish landlords, anxious to get rid of buildings too costly to maintain, claimed the renewal meant progress. Both sides agreed to arbitration by the rabbinical court. After long proceedings a solution was found which was accepted by both parties. The owners sold their property to the renewal authority, which in turn passed it over to a tenants' council to operate and manage and eventually sell to the tenants themselves. Much of the negotiations were handled by Rabbi Korff. While studying the points and charges of that issue, he came up with another, far-reaching proposal: a Landlord–Tenant Community Relations Court to resolve many of the problems that face the poor in heavily-populated urban centers. His thinking—and pushing—ultimately led to the establishment of the state's Housing Court in 1973.

The rabbinical court in Boston represents sixty-five congregations that include most of the 250,000 Jews in Massachusetts. Made up of six or so rabbis from the area, it comprises all three branches of Judaism, unlike the other rabbinical courts in the country, most of which are Orthodox.

Disputants need not be Jewish to seek resolutions from the beth din (house of law). "Justice has no creed, race or religion," Rabbi Korff says. He then cites the example of a tenant who leases an apartment and then finds it has cracks in the walls and holes in the floor. He has signed the lease, but who is liable? Rabbi Korff concludes that Jewish law says the landlord must make every repair because "no one has the right to sell something that is a receptacle for human misery."

The Columbia Journal of Law and Social Problems, writing about rabbinical courts, sees great potential for them in solving modern-day social conflicts:

> Although there are numerous advantages in using rabbinical courts, only a very small percentage of Jews actually utilize them. One reason is that these courts are virtually unknown to the vast majority of their potential users. More publicity for the court and its work would provide a partial solution to this problem. One possibility would be reporting of rabbinical court decisions in local newspapers, as is done by the Jewish Conciliation Board.*

> While the scope of the rabbinical courts' subject matter jurisdiction is virtually unlimited as long as all parties submit to it, the courts deal mainly with family and small personal problems. Yet, as can be seen in the Boston case, the court can be extremely helpful in matters of larger social concern. . . . For example, instead of going to the landlord, to civil courts or to the police, tenants who have complaints against their co-tenants for offenses such as excessive noise, throwing garbage out the window, and other similar matters, could go to a rabbinical court for a solution. While this would be especially helpful in large housing projects or cooperatives that are predominately Jewish, the procedure could also be used with tenants of different religions . . . as long as both parties voluntarily submit to the court's jurisdiction.

There is no charge to landlord or tenant using either a rabbinical court or the arbitration of a single rabbi and, as stated earlier, neither side need be Jewish.

---

* A private arbitration agency that serves the New York metropolitan area. The JCB, non-denominational in its services, offers arbitration before a panel that includes a rabbi, a lawyer, a businessman and a psychiatrist. They are now expanding their procedure, calling in specialists in various fields. There is no charge to tenants or landlords.

Rabbi Wolfe Kelman, executive head of the Conservative Rabbinical Society and a frequent ("*too* many cases") arbitrator, states: "People say 'let's not wash our dirty linen in court, we'll go to the rabbi.'" There are other pluses. Although it has taken on some tough, major housing cases, rabbinical arbitration works particularly well for the individual tenant and the small landlord and in cases where the issues are more moral and intangible than monetary and rigidly defined, such as harassment, possible discrimination, or promised repairs. For these people the rabbinical procedure might appear less intimidating (and of course it is less costly) than that of the structured American Arbitration Association. Many rabbis do, however, follow AAA procedure at their hearings.

Opinions of arbitration hearings tend to hinge on who emerged victorious. If the consumer wins, businesses tend to say that awards are *always* made to the customer; when the consumer wins a portion, but not all, of what he was claiming, he too is sometimes disgruntled. But talking the problem out helps, as does the fact that at last a final resolution of a long-standing conflict has been reached.

Utilizing the media

Everyone enjoys good human interest stories. Newspapers and television news programs welcome them to balance the heavier news of the day. Readers/viewers cheer or weep over them. Tenants can use them to special advantage.

Naturally news editors are not going to be interested in one tenant's hassle with the landlord over a wheezing refrigerator (unless he shoots him!), but here is what *will* get you or your tenant group publicity that, hopefully, will bring about a favorable settlement of your dispute.

A couple bought a puppy for their nine-year-old son who was

confined to a wheelchair. A year later the owner of their small apartment building arbitrarily decreed "no pets." The couple appealed to local newspapers. As you can imagine, they ran wrenching stories on the boy and his dog. What could the villainous landlord do? "Awright, he can keep the #%!? dog."

In Manhattan a tenant group protesting management's refusal to make repairs on their building hung bed sheets from the windows with the enormous hand-painted message: "This building is a lemon." They even drew a huge lemon on the banner. The press loved that one. The landlord was interviewed. He promised repairs. And an editorial eye was kept on the scene for followup stories.

As you see, in order to interest assignment desks your problem will have to be an offbeat one and/or make for good picture taking—unless the apartment house itself is famous. What organized tenants do in the Hancock Tower in Chicago, for instance, is always news because the building itself is distinctive— architecturally significant, unusual design of apartments over shop and office levels, and so on. New York's Co-op City is also newsworthy because it is the largest cooperative community in the world. Residents' dissatisfaction with security in the complex, or with rising maintenance charges is almost a "beat" reporting job. But if your building is ordinary, you will somehow have to make it extraordinary. As the line in *Gypsy* goes, "You gotta have a gimmick." Hand-painted sheets blowing in the wind for a day or two, although perhaps aesthetically offensive, was a tactic that worked for the New York group. With a little thought your tenant group should be able to come up with something equally attention getting.

The beauty of press attention is that, in the interest of objective journalism, it forces reporters to talk to your opponent for his side of the issue. If he is 100 percent in the wrong, his weak defense will be apparent in the story. He will know it. And nobody wants to appear foolish or unethical in front of the entire community. If the landlord's conduct is also technically outside the law, the publicity is much worse. In either event, he would be wise to straighten things out and get himself off the front pages fast.

If you prefer to skirt the hard news columns, consumerism has seen the rise of helpful newspaper features such as "Action Line" or "Help!" and local radio and television reporters who also seek satisfaction for consumer complaints. Try them—the newspapers for more mundane landlord gripes, radio and television for dramatic problems and those involving the entire building, not just a lone tenant.

Or do you need a lawyer?

There are instances when none of the above-mentioned suggestions will work and you will have to retain a lawyer:

• If you have a problem that hasn't been solved or made clearer by reading this book. In this case perhaps one consultation with a lawyer will be all that is needed to set you straight. You should be able to talk with a lawyer for this kind of advice for a $15–$35 fee.

• If your landlord is suing you for a good deal of money.

• If you are suing for a great deal of money. If, for example, you slipped on a banana peel in the lobby, broke both legs and are seeking a judgment many, many times the amount you could be awarded in small claims court.

• If you and your fellow tenants have just organized over a number of problems with the building and are about to begin a rent strike until conditions are remedied. You may not need a lawyer, if you live in an area with a strong, local tenant group to guide you through the strike. If you don't, counsel is vital, for rent withholding is grounds for eviction and must be properly handled if it is to stay within the law. A lawyer is even more important if your strike will be conducted *outside* the law.

• If you've moved into a new condominium and are awash in the developer's broken promises. He is building many more units than were advertised, there are no plans for a swimming pool despite a glossy picture of one in the sales brochure, and there aren't enough parking spaces. You and the other unit-owners should consult a lawyer if you plan to sue the developer.

Lawyers *are* expensive. Most charge fees in a range of $30 to $50 an hour. Clearly when your dispute with the landlord involves a few hundred dollars it would make better sense to try other means of settlement first.

But if your case is similar to the ones mentioned above, you cannot avoid hiring a lawyer. How do you find one? Well, if you are very poor you may qualify for help from a Legal Aid office. Call your County Clerk's office for the location of the office nearest you. If you will have to pay for legal services, ask your friends or your local tenant or consumer group for the names of attorneys they could recommend. Actually the latter organizations are probably better since they may have lawyers on their staff who are, naturally, familiar with landlord–tenant law, while your friends may recommend attorneys whose specialty might be, say, admiralty law.

Lawyers' fees vary, depending on age, reputation, special expertise in the field and the nature of the case. Sometimes you will pay by the hour, sometimes by the case. Negligence case fees, for example, are contingent on a lawyer's winning the case, so they are rather high, ranging between 25 and 50 percent of the settlement.

One new development that may ease the pinch of fee payments is prepaid legal services, which does for legal problems what Blue Cross and Blue Shield do for subscribers who become ill: It pays the lawyer with funds that have been withheld previously from the subscriber's paycheck.

The plan now operates in labor unions and other organizations in several states. In Shreveport, Louisiana, for one, prepaid legal aid is available to members of the International Laborers Union. The cost to the individual worker is about $40 per family per year. The subscriber has the right to choose any lawyer for advice or court representation in most civil and almost all criminal proceedings (for fees ranging from $100 to $325) whether he is filing the action himself or is being sued. The plan for another union, this one in California, runs about $3.75 a month for three hours of legal services, generally office consultation, to $10 a month for sixty hours of legal work, which would include court litigation. There is no one nationwide program; terms of the plans vary from one state to another. At this writing there are some 2,500 insurance programs in operation around the country.

As a last resort, if your problems with the landlord appear insoluble, you might simply move out. There are conditions that would permit you to do this in the middle of the lease agreement without first notifying the landlord that you are doing so. One example would be a rat infestation. In fact, in such a situation you could not only break a lease, but you can also sue the landlord for money damages, including movers' charges. You'll need a lawyer to handle such a suit.

CHAPTER 13

□

What to Buy and
Where to Write for
Still More Information

Tenants–General

Landlords and Tenants: A Complete Guide to the Residential Rental Relationship by Jerome G. Rose. E. P. Dutton. 1973. $9.75 cloth, $3.95 paper. A comprehensive reference guide to landlord–tenant law governing rents, leases, public housing, condominiums, cooperatives, strikes, tenant unions. Mr. Rose, an attorney and professor of Urban Planning at Rutgers University, impartially analyzes the rights of both parties to the rental agreement.

Landlord-Tenant Relationships—A Selected Bibliography. 1971. Price: 60¢. A U.S. Department of Housing and Urban Development booklet available from the Superintendent of Documents, U.S. Government Printing Office, Washington, D.C. 20402. (When writing for publications from the Superintendent of Documents in Washington, D.C., allow ten weeks for delivery.) This booklet is also available from a regional Government Printing Office bookstore. This bibliography, although already somewhat dated in a rapidly changing arena, should prove helpful to tenant unions and other groups seeking to organize. Listings include books and magazine articles on landlord-tenant procedures and problems, names and addresses of major regional tenant and housing organizations.

Tenants and the Urban Housing Crisis, edited by Stephen Burghardt. The New Press, Dexter, Michigan. 1972. $3.95. A compilation of articles, some of which appeared in other publications, by a variety of people in the housing field. Heavy emphasis on tenant organizing, with case histories of tenant movements and rent strikes, their strategies and successes.

The *National Tenants Organization* publishes no booklets for tenants, in part because of a lack of funds, but principally because rents and rent control laws, eviction grounds, and so forth differ from state to state, making a pamphlet for a national readership impracticable. The NTO will, however, answer any question a tenant may have and can put him or her in touch with the appropriate government agency or tenant group in his or her area for more specific inquiries. Some state housing authorities or tenant organizations publish directories for apartment dwellers in their region on all phases of the rental relationship, although these are usually in the subsidized housing area, as indeed is most of the work of the NTO.

The NTO publishes a monthly newsletter, "Tenants Outlook." Subscription price is $3 a year for tenants, $12 for non-tenants (such as government agencies or media). The National Tenants Organization is at 425 Thirteenth Street, N.W., Washington, D.C. 20005. Telephone (202) 347-3358.

California Tenants Handbook by Myron Moskovitz, Ralph E. Warner and Charles E. Sherman. Nolo Press, Berkeley, Calif. 1972. $3.95. Three California attorneys guide tenants through the rental labyrinth in that state. Every facet of the rental agreement/lease is explored, from how to cope with eviction to getting repairs made. Though written for California apartment dwellers, the handbook offers explanations of terms and tips for handling oneself when dealing with the landlord that could apply anywhere in the country.

* * *

The Tenant Survival Book by Emily Jane Goodman. Bobbs-Merrill. 1972. $8.50 cloth, $3.95 soft cover. New American Library Paperback $1.95. An attorney, Ms. Goodman focuses on landlord-tenant law. Much of the manual—the chapter on squatters, for example—is directed to the poor, but woven throughout the sometimes radical rhetoric is solid information for higher-income groups too. Chapters cover an explanation of the economics of the landlord-tenant system, strikes, the courts, collective bargaining, lawyers and tenant unions.

Super Tenant: Your Legal Rights and How to Use Them by John M. Striker and Andrew O. Shapiro. Brownstone Publishers, Inc., New York. 1973. $2.95. A handbook strictly for the New York City tenant by two legal minds. Answers the usual spate of tenant queries, with special attention paid to regional information on rent control, rent stabilization and vacancy decontrol in the city.

A Shopper's Guide to Lawyers by Herbert S. Denenberg, Pennsylvania Insurance Commissioner. How do you choose a lawyer? And how much can you expect to pay for his or her services? Mr. Denenberg sets guidelines for the consumer. For example: "Don't rely on lawyer reference services." The guide is available by sending a self-addressed stamped (20¢ worth) envelope to the Pennsylvania Insurance Department, Finance Building, Harrisburg, Pa. 17180.

How to Pass Legislation by Pine Tree Legal Assistance, Inc., with the assistance of the League of Women Voters. Excellent explanation of the legislative process for groups preparing bills for submission. Covers sponsorship, lobbying, hearings, drumming up local support. Available for 50¢ from Pine Tree Legal Assistance, Inc., 565 Congress Street, Portland, Maine 04101.

SOURCE Catalog: Communities/Housing. Swallow Press. 1972. $7.00 cloth, $2.95 paper. Bibliography of reports, articles, status of legislation, tenant groups, and brief definitions of problems in the housing area. Basically for renters, but makes mention of mobile-home owners and urban homesteaders. Book should be especially helpful to tenant unions and to public housing, third world and other tenants in special circumstances—squatters, the elderly, and those in need of day care—to whom particular attention is paid. SOURCE, the group that compiled the book, appears to be a coalition of many housing, community, educational and other organizations. Order from the Swallow Press, Inc., 1139 S. Wabash Ave., Chicago, Illinois 60605 or from SOURCE, P. O. Box 21066, Washington, D.C. 20009.

Less Rent and More Control: A Tenant's Guide to Rent Control in Massachusetts by The Community Research and Publications Group. Available from Urban Planning Aid, Inc., 639 Massachusetts Avenue, Cambridge, Mass. 02139. 1973. $1.50 to individuals; $3.00 to official agencies. Describes Massachusetts rent control laws, procedures for getting rent control legislation passed, problems after passage and enforcement. Directed to tenant groups, lawyers, and other housing activists.

Apartment hunting

The Apartment Finder's Handbook by Robert Ross. Taurus Communications, New York. 1971. $3.95. For New York tenants only. What to look for, description of specific New York neighborhoods, listing of buildings by address, name of managing agent and nitty-gritty rating by its tenants.

Condominiums and cooperatives

Condominiums and Cooperatives by David Clurman, Assistant New York State Attorney General in charge of cooperative and condominium regulation, and Edna L. Hebard, Associate Professor of Business Administration, Indiana University. Wiley-Interscience. 1970. $15.00. This is the definitive book on the two housing methods by one of the country's leading authorities on the subject and is aimed at the developer, the would-be buyer, and the housing specialist. Sample chapter headings: "Legal Structure of a Condominium," "Assessing a Community," "Institutional Financing of Condominiums," "Should a Home Buyer Purchase a Condominium?" "Operation and Management of Condominium Regime," "Cooperatives: Operations, Legal Structure, Purchases and Sales."

The Condominium Buyer's Guide by James N. Karr. Frederick Fell Publishers, New York. 1973. $9.95. The book is divided into two sections: "Understanding the Condominium Concept" and "Choosing the Right Condominium." The latter half takes the prospective buyer step-by-step through the purchase of year-round and vacation condos. Much information on financing and helping the reader to understand the financial obligation of condominium ownership.

The First International Guide on How to Purchase a Condominium or Vacation/Retirement Home by Jerome E. Klein and Glenn Fowler. Lehigh Books, New York. 1973. $3.95. As the title says, a how-to-buy manual with special emphasis on buying into developments in Europe, Mexico, and the Caribbean.

Condominiums—Their Development & Management by Anthony D. Grezzo. A publication of the Office of International Affairs, Department of Housing & Urban Development. 1972. $1.25. Available from Superintendent of Documents, U. S. Government Printing Office, Washington, D.C. 20402. A seventy-page study designed to inform interested persons and institutions on the United States system of developing and financing a condominium. Appendix offers model master deeds, bylaws, operating budget, subscription and purchase agreement, management agreement.

Townhouses & Condominiums: Residents' Likes and Dislikes by Dr. Carl Norcross. A special report of the Urban Land Institute. 105 pages. 1973. Available from ULI–the Urban Land Institute,

1200 18th Street, N.W., Washington, D.C. 20036. Cost to non-members: $15; to members: $12. How are new owners finding the condominium experience? Dr. Norcross surveys residents in forty-nine condominium and townhouse projects in California and the Washington, D.C. area. Owners are asked about their overall satisfaction with the development, the density of the project, its design, parking problems, recreation facilities, homeowner associations, and other areas of tenant (dis)satisfaction.

Condominium Listing Information Center. Thinking of moving to a Florida condominium? This is a clearing house for developments located from Miami to Palm Beach *only.* There are display areas for developers, decorators, furniture makers and other professionals with an interest in that housing style. The center is meant for on-premises visiting, but mail information about the various condominium projects in the area will be sent if the writer is specific about his or her needs. If you ask about developments in the $35,000–$40,000 price range, for instance, you will receive a prompt response. A request for "general information about Florida condominiums" will get you a form letter asking for specifics. The staff at the "Condo Center" is there to give information; they are not salespeople. "Not shilling for anybody" is the way one of the partners in the venture put it. The Condominium Listing Information Center is at 201st Street & Biscayne Boulevard, Miami, Florida 33160.

Managing a Successful Community Association, a report published jointly by the Urban Land Institute and the Community Associations Institute. Cost is $10 (or $5 each in quantities of five or more). This is a guide directed toward aiding board members, committee chairmen, property managers, lawyers and volunteers involved in running a condominium or townhouse association. The book covers every aspect of association work from procedures for handling cash receipts to how to organize a spaghetti supper. Available from ULI—the Urban Land Institute, 1200 18th Street, N.W., Washington, D.C. 20036.

* * *

Condominiums USA & Homes Overseas. A bimonthly magazine printed in England and distributed around the world. Varied editorial matter interspersed with heavy advertising for condominium communities and brokers here and abroad. Typical chapters in one issue: "The Recreational Lease—Is It Right?," "The Condominium Comes of Age in Florida," "Teenager Adjustment to a Planned Community." Price: $2 a copy, $12 per year. Write Condominiums USA & Homes Overseas, Inc., 50 Union Avenue, Irvington, N.J. 07111.

Cooperative leaflets

If you and your fellow tenants are interested in buying your building from the landlord and turning it into a cooperative, David Clurman, Assistant Attorney General in charge of condominiums and cooperatives for the State of New York, can start you on the path to conversion. His office publishes a leaflet outlining conversion requirements that will be sent without charge to any bona fide tenant group in or out of New York State. Although written for New Yorkers, many of the sheet's tips are applicable to would-be cooperators anywhere. Write the Office of the Assistant New York State Attorney General in charge of Cooperative and Condominium Regulation, Two World Trade Center, New York, N.Y. 10047. Ask for Form CPS-3.

The Cooperative League of the USA is a national organization of health, credit, farm marketing, consumer goods and housing cooperatives. They have a number of books and pamphlets available on, among other subjects, organizing food-buying clubs and credit unions and the workings of a housing cooperative. Sample titles: "Primer of Bookkeeping for Cooperatives" ($1.75), "Co-op Stores and Buying Clubs" (free), "Plus Values in Cooperative Housing" (25¢) and "Moving Ahead With Group Action," subtitled "Effective Self-Help—The Buying Club: A First Step in Consumer Group Action" (85¢). For a list of other available publications, write Cooperative League of the USA, 1828 L St. N.W., Washington, D.C. 20036.

A Primer for the Members of the Board of Directors in Housing Cooperatives by the Mutual Ownership Development Foundation. Breaks down the responsibilities and duties of board members and their committees. Send 20¢ in postage to M.O.D. Foundation, 681 Market Street, San Francisco, California 94105.

Security

Try your local public library for a copy of the February, 1971 *Consumer Reports*. The issue contains a special 10-page section on door locks, including a detailed discussion on locks in general and ratings of the tested locks grouped by types. The article is also included in the *Consumer Reports 1973 Buying Guide*. For a copy by mail send a check for $2.65 to *Consumer Reports*, P. O. Box 1111, Mount Vernon, N.Y. 10550.

Defensible Space by Oscar Newman. The Macmillan Company. 1972. Cloth $8.95; paper $2.95. Widely publicized theory of how physical design factors in public housing are building crime into the projects. Architect and planner Newman studies and criticizes several New York complexes that are not "defensible" for their tenants and offers design solutions.

Being Safe by Mel Mandell. Saturday Review Press. 1972. Cloth, $6.95; Paperback Library $1.50. How to protect your home (a special chapter on apartment house security), your car, your office. The author thoroughly investigates locks and alarm systems from the simplest chain latch to the most sophisticated electronic security system.

How to Conduct a Campaign for Better Street Lighting in Your Community. Pamphlet available from Street and Highway Safety Lighting Bureau, 1212 Avenue of the Americas, New York, New York 10036. No charge.

Twenty-Two Steps to Safer Neighborhoods. Suggestions for fighting crime individually and with a group. Examples given of such programs in action as escort patrols; volunteer receptionists in police precincts; protection of social security checks; block watchers and Community Radio Watch Programs. Available from The National Alliance for Safer Cities, 165 East 56 Street, New York, New York 10022. No charge for single copies. Bulk orders of 10 or more, 15¢ for each booklet.

Accident, Automotive and Burglar Protection. Underwriters' Laboratories, Inc., a seventy-nine-year-old nonprofit organization that tests electrical products to make certain they meet national safety standards, offers this booklet containing a complete listing of all burglar alarm systems approved by UL. For a copy, send $1.00 to:

> Underwriters' Laboratories, Inc.
> Publications Department
> 207 East Ohio Street
> Chicago, Ill. 60611

Roaches and rats

Cockroaches—How to Control Them, issued by U. S. Department of Agriculture. Write Superintendent of Documents, U.S. Government Printing Office, Washington, D.C. 20402. Cost is 10¢. Rather dated and doubts the efficacy of boric acid powder, but the booklet does contain interesting drawings of the insects so you can see which species inhabit your kitchen, which species are in the bathroom, which . . . .

Control of Domestic Rats & Mice, produced by the U.S. Department of Health, Education and Welfare. Available from Superintendent of Documents, U.S. Government Printing Office, Washington, D.C. 20402. Price: 50¢. The forty-two-page booklet covers all aspects of rodent problems in multifamily dwellings: description and habits of domestic rodents, control, sanitation, ratproofing the building and the organization of community rat control problems. There is even a chapter on "carcass disposal."

Tenant organizing

New Jersey Tenants Organization Organizing Manual. Eight-page guide to setting up a tenant association. Directed toward New Jersey apartment dwellers, but useful by analogy to renters outside the state. Write New Jersey Tenants Organization, P. O. Box 1142, Fort Lee, N.J. 07024. No charge, but it would be thoughtful to include a stamped self-addressed envelope.

Newsletters

For ideas on design, the National Tenants Organization will send fledgling editors two or three copies of typical newsletters that office receives. And that's more than 300 bulletins a month! The National Tenants Organization is at 425 Thirteenth Street, N.W., Washington, D.C. 20005.

Small Claims Court

Sue the B*st*rds by Douglas Matthews. Arbor House. 1973. $2.95. Readable, informative consumer guide to suing in Small Claims Court. The only information author Matthews appears to have omitted is which states offer "how to sue" manuals and maps to their various courts compiled by their own consumer affairs departments. Perhaps he thought that data would compete with his own book. But what government-printed booklet would advise older women plaintiffs to "avoid net stockings, sloppy hats, gigantic pocketbooks and the like, especially in combination with one another. . . . There is an equation in the judicial mind that says 'kooky dress—kooky broad.' The Julie look rather than the Tricia look, and avoid Zazu Pitts at all costs."

Several states *do* offer no-charge printed information on the workings of their Small Claims Courts. To see if your state does, contact the Department of Consumer Affairs of the state Attorney General's office or your state's Public Interest Resource Group.

The following booklets offer addresses of courts, maps, and other information for area residents:

"How to Sue in Small Claims Court in New York City"
Department of Consumer Affairs
80 Lafayette Street
New York, N.Y. 10013
(Available in English and Spanish)

"Your Small Claims Court"
Legal Aid Society of Santa Clara County
235 E. Santa Clara Street
San Jose, Calif. 95112
(Available in English and Spanish)

"How to File a Suit in the New Jersey Small Claims Division"
Office of Public Information
New Jersey Community Affairs Department
P. O. Box 2768
Trenton, N.J. 08625

"How to Sue in Small Claims Court"
Division of Consumer Services
Florida Department of Agriculture and Consumer Services
Center Building
Tallahassee, Fla. 32301

"Small Claims Fact Sheet"
Consumer Protection
Department of Justice
State Capitol Building
Madison, Wis. 53702

"How to Sue in Small Claims Court in Western Massachusetts"
Western Massachusetts Public Interest Resource Group
233 North Pleasant Street, Suite 30
Amherst, Mass. 01002

"How to Sue in Small Claims Court"
Seattle Legal Services Center
Central Area Office
2401 South Jackson Street
Seattle, Wash. 98144

"A Guide to the Connecticut Small Claims Courts"
Department of Consumer Protection
State Office Building
Hartford, Conn. 06115

Consumer groups

Information for Consumers, compiled by the staff of "Everybody's
Money," the quarterly publication of the National Credit Union
Administration, lists state consumer groups, government agencies
and the names and addresses of the presidents of service/product
firms. The forty-eight-page booklet is available for 50¢ from
Information for Consumers, Dept. EM, Box 431, Madison, Wis.
53701.

Arbitration

The American Arbitration Association offers a raft of printed material on arbitration as a means of dispute settlement. Write The American Arbitration Association, 140 West 51 Street, New York, N.Y. 10020. There is no charge for any of the association's publications.

The National Center for Dispute Settlement, an arm of the AAA, has published the booklet "Professional Services in the Resolution of Disputes." It is available at no charge from the National Center for Dispute Settlement, 1212–1214 Sixteenth St., N.W., Washington, D.C. 20036.

Index